MW01699736

NEVER *Give Up*

To Vicky

Remember you are never alone.

Joan Care

GLOBAL PUBLISHING GROUP

Global Publishing Group
Australia • New Zealand • Singapore • America • London

NEVER Give Up

7 Powerful Secrets I Learnt from my Famous Friends & How They Can Transform Your Life!

Foreword by Elyse Taylor

JeanClare

DISCLAIMER

All the information, techniques, skills and concepts contained within this publication are of the nature of general comment only and are not in any way recommended as individual advice. The intent is to offer a variety of information to provide a wider range of choices now and in the future, recognising that we all have widely diverse circumstances and viewpoints. Should any reader choose to make use of the information contained herein, this is their decision, and the contributors (and their companies), authors and publishers do not assume any responsibilities whatsoever under any condition or circumstances. It is recommended that the reader obtain their own independent advice.

First Edition 2017

National Library of Australia
Cataloguing-in-Publication entry:

Creator: JeanClare, author.

Title: Never Give Up: 7 Powerful Secrets I Learnt from my Famous
Friends & How They Can Transform Your Life! / JeanClare.

1st ed.
ISBN: 9781925288537 (paperback)

Self-actualization (Psychology)
Spiritual healing
Self-help techniques

Published by Global Publishing Group
PO Box 517 Mt Evelyn, Victoria 3796 Australia
Email info@GlobalPublishingGroup.com.au

Printed in China

For further information about orders:
Phone: +61 3 9739 4686 or Fax +61 3 8648 6871

This book is dedicated with thanks to my
Angel Clare, my family and clients for
the extraordinary life I have lived and
experienced because of your faith and
belief in who I am.

Also thank you to Darren Stephens for
opening the door for my dream to
become a reality.

JeanClare

ACKNOWLEDGEMENTS

I acknowledge with love and gratitude the many people who made this book possible. My special clients whom I hold dear to my heart, who shared their lives with me and trusted my insight and guidance; Miranda Kerr for her grace and dignity, Orlando Bloom for his respect, Yael Lilienfeld for her courage, Pete Everett for his transformation, Jeannine Kaspar for her commitment and continued friendship, Elyse Taylor for her high standards of integrity and trust, and Luke Gottwald for his inspiring passion and ability to never give up.

My many wonderful clients from around the world shared their lives with me and inspired me to write this book by constantly requesting information and knowledge on self-transformation. Thank you to everyone at Global Publishing; without you this book would not exist.

Thank-you to my amazing and wonderful children who are a constant source of encouragement and motivation, who never stop believing in me. To some special friends, Andrew Beasley, Rob Mcdonell, Rhonda Cannon and Andy Yeates, I must acknowledge your unshakable belief in me as a human and friend.

With love and laughter always,

JeanClare

FREE BONUS GIFT

We can't give you everything you need to know about living an inspirational and transformational life in one small book.

So we've created a very special website with loads of extra goodies, just for you.

To gain instant access to these **FREE** resources, simply visit this website:

www.NeverGiveUpJeanClare.com

CONTENTS

FOREWORD

JeanClare provided me with light when I was surrounded by darkness.

I truly believe that there are no coincidences in life and if this book has ended up in your lap, it's for a reason.

Jeannie's words and foresight helped give me the self-empowerment to trust my intuition and make incredibly difficult decisions to create my own happiness, not only for myself but for my daughter.

This book is designed to allow you to rediscover your true passion, to get clear about what you really want in life and to give you a new way of focusing your mind.

I'm proud to recommend this book. Its author JeanClare is a leading expert with over 30 years of experience. JeanClare has taken on the ultimate challenge and continues to grow professionally and personally.

This is truly an inspiring read and one that will make you want to step out of your comfort zone and take action.

And I encourage you to do just that!

Elyse Taylor

INTRODUCTION

This book is about transformation, freedom and finding the other person inside you that has been hiding since you were born.

Every now and then you will see glimpses of him/her and you will feel motivated, happy and do amazing things. Then what happens? He/she disappears and you go back to living your old life with a few added bonuses. Then one morning you wake up and say to yourself, "I can't live like this anymore." You will probably blame your career choice or a family member or maybe both. My insights are a guide to help you find yourself. Please take the information for what it is. I don't claim to have all the answers and leave it up to you to take from this book what is right for you, as I sincerely believe that there is a greater force out there in the universe that will provide the information you need at a time that is perfect for you.

The words are written in gratitude to every client I have worked with over the past 30 years who have believed, stayed focused and never given up. You often sent me a thank you for the clarity, enlightenment and motivation, but it is me who is thanking you for pushing me to a place where I have constantly had to step up to the next level to stay one step ahead of you all. I have peeled away the layers of my invented life to share with you the results so that you can create transformation in days or weeks, and not take 30 years as I did to find the answer.

The teachings and inspiration of my words will hopefully remind you of what you already know and may have forgotten, just accept what feels right for you and allow the insight to awaken your inner knowing. Trust yourself and allow the belief that every piece of information you need sits on the edge of your reality, waiting for your acceptance.

Inside this story are the inspirations, education and knowledge that I have learned and experienced with some incredibly famous people, who are all very special to me. I will help you transform your life and create your dreams. Some of the information you may not want to hear but I promise, it will make a difference to how you think and feel about yourself and others. I know this book will not suit everyone, but if you have picked it up, then it's a sign. Start the journey now.

We are all unique and different in some way, but we are also very similar in many ways. We are human.

Start the journey now. Accept my invitation to you to find yourself.

THE POWER OF SEVEN

WE ALL KNOW THERE ARE:

Seven levels of healing

Seven layers to the Aura

Seven colours to the Chakras

Seven Major Chakras in the body

Seven unique musical notes, one for each Chakra

Seven colours in a rainbow

Seven steps to happiness

Seven secrets to success

Seven Archangels

Seven Dwarves

When I decided to write this book, I promised myself that it would not be just another book of information like so many other books out there. I stopped reading self-help books a long time ago because they always told me what I should do and how I should be acting to create what I want. Not many told me how or why I do what I do when I am in the space of sabotaging my life, or why I felt happy one day and not the next. Let's face it, we all do it. I have found that the very wealthy people in the world often have a miserable family or private life because they don't know how to balance their emotions or recognise who they are in all situations. The business men work 24/7 because that's where they feel powerful, successful, admired and appreciated. When they need to deal with family or relationships they are in denial or at a loss as to how to do both. Some of you are amazing at home and family or being creative, spiritual and caring for the world but your finances are not so healthy.

I am offering you an opportunity to find your other person inside yourself, so you know what is holding you back, sabotaging your life and making you feel how you do on a bad day. With these tools, you can create amazing motivation, life focus and clarity. YOU WILL NEED TO COMMIT TO YOURSELF. No one can do it for you. It needs to be a lifelong commitment. I believe we have seven personality traits that have cause and effect. The seven traits are the positive and negative aspects of who we believe we are and how we behave toward our self and those around us.

If we are not in harmony with our mind body spirit, we cannot have harmony in our everyday lives.

SEVEN SECRETS TO SUCCESS

1. Grace and Dignity .... Miranda Kerr
2. Courage.. Yael Lilienfeld
3. Transformation .... Pete Everett/John Scott
4. Commitment.. Jeannine Kaspar
5. Integrity .... Elyse Taylor
6. Respect... Orlando Bloom
7. Passion .... Luke Gottwald

Without grace and dignity there can be no courage; without courage there can be no transformation; without transformation there is no commitment; without commitment there is no integrity; without integrity there can be no respect; without respect there can be no passion. Without passion, there is no inner peace, success or reason to exist.

Chapter 1

GRACE AND DIGNITY

Miranda Kerr

Chapter 1

GRACE AND DIGNITY

Miranda Kerr

People with grace and dignity usually know what they want and don't let the negative influences of other people stop them from creating their dreams. They are very strong yet gentle people.

A few obvious people with grace and dignity:

Jacqueline Lee "Jackie" Kennedy Onassis

Sir Richard Branson

Barack Obama

Michelle Obama

Dick Smith

Jennifer Hawkins

Miranda Kerr

Tom Hanks

Helen Mirren

Hugh Jackman

Nicole Kidman

Nelson Mandela

Mother Teresa

Diana Spencer (Princess of Wales)

They don't react emotionally because they are not angry inside. They present themselves to the world as clear, tolerant and dignified people. They do not react to public pressure and act out for the media or anyone else; they treat everyone they meet with equality, grace and dignity which means they treat themselves with Grace and Dignity.

GRACE AND DIGNITY

I met Miranda Kerr in 2008. As soon as I spent time with her, I knew she was unique. There is a wisdom that radiates from her that most humans don't embrace after experiencing a 100 lifetimes. This wisdom enhances her grace and dignity and though she is a gentle, loving soul, she certainly has a powerful inner strength and knows her own mind. Her choices are made from the heart with courage, dignity and consideration for herself and those around her. I have met lots of famous and beautiful people but Miranda has a special inner beauty that radiates from her heart to all areas of her life. She exudes confidence and happiness.

I believe grace and dignity is one of her secrets to success. No matter who she is with or what she is doing, there is always an element of excitement around her. Miranda readily shares her open, loving and caring personality with everyone she meets no matter who they are. She has no fear of being herself and allowing her beautiful light to shine through because she lives her life on every level with grace and dignity. Her unique ability to understand herself and those around her, opens the door for inner peace and happiness. The total acceptance of herself and her ability to be elegant in every aspect of her life, is enhanced by her commitment to taking care of herself on all levels, physically, spiritually, mentally and emotionally. Always quick to smile and embrace new possibilities, Miranda always shines and is the perfect example of grace, elegance and dignity. As I spent time with her, I realised that she had no anger. I believe this is partly because she does not hold onto the past and always works hard to have a better future for herself and her family. She loves everyone in her life and is happy from the inside.

Just because it is not naturally part of your personality it doesn't mean you can't learn how to embrace that way of being. Once you start your spiritual journey, there is no turning back. It just doesn't happen that way. Miranda started her journey a long time ago and every day she does something to ensure her life stays on track. It may be yoga, clean eating or just being happy. She also has the knowledge that the past belongs there and the future is an adventure to be grateful for. She does not hold on to anger or resentment; she gets on with life always looking forward with passion, hope and a strong belief that all will be exactly how it is meant to be.

To live with grace and dignity one needs to be free of anger, jealousy or resentment. Keep reading and you can find out how to have grace and dignity in your life as a tool for success. A clear and balanced mind is the key. I know as I spent time with Miranda she developed her own spirituality and intuition and I guided her to have clarity in many of her life situations. Her generous nature was unwavering and I will be forever grateful for the experiences I shared with her and her family. She allowed me access to experiences I would never had known if she had not been the person she is. I attended Victoria Secret fashion parade, David Jones winter and spring showings, amazing lunches and dinners with her family, the privilege of teaching her and her family Reiki, accommodation with Miranda and Orlando in Los Angeles and a lot of other privileged experiences.

The most important experience with Miranda was the way she treated people in her life. I was privileged to be able to see her in action with all different sorts of staff, from her PA, hairdressers, makeup artists, agents, house cleaners, gardeners, to her beautiful Nan and Pop Kerr. She treated everyone with the same charm and friendship, making everyone feel welcome and appreciated.

> “Anger is a wind which blows out the lamp of the mind.”
>
> ROBERT GREEN INGERSOLL

“ONCE YOU GIVE UP ANGER YOU OPEN THE DOOR FOR YOUR SUBCONSCIOUS TO CREATE ANYTHING YOUR HEART DESIRES.”

JeanClare

Working with Miranda on her journey of self-empowerment allowed me to embrace my own gifts and knowledge. Being in the presence of such a gifted person opened the doors for me to embrace every aspect of who I am as a person and to understand that what I do is a profession, not a label. I have the choice of living two lives, one as the person I choose to be in my career and the other person, me, the human. How I represent myself with my work will also reflect on my personal life and to a certain extent govern my behaviour and actions but what I do as a career choice is not who I am.

This is my little story of how I discovered I was angry, it wasn't evident to me or anyone else because I always appeared to be happy, but a secret part of me had it all locked away in a very deep place.

I have always been a quiet person avoiding verbal or physical confrontation of any kind. I relate this back to my childhood and my mother's reaction to her own life situation which she couldn't handle, so she became verbally and physically abusive. I decided at a very early age if I was going to survive I needed to become invisible. If no one could see me then I would be safe. Little did I realise as a child that it was my spirit and my belief in myself that became invisible. I realise now that she was not angry with me, she was just frustrated and felt disappointed with her own life. As I came to understand her pain, I released my own need to feel disappointed because my mother didn't understand who I was or how to treat me. I gave up the lie that it was about me, which I took on because of the way she sometimes treated me. Her behaviour was a representation of her fears for me, that my life might finish up like hers. My freedom came from forgiving myself for not being the perfect daughter, letting go of the guilt of not being and doing what I thought my mother wanted me to do. I realised that I needed to be myself, not the creation of my mother or anyone else, and that I was not responsible for her.

As I stepped back and looked at the foundation of my anger, I realised that I didn't understand myself and yet I expected everyone else to understand me and fix my life. As I was faced with my own need to escape the emotional prison I had built for myself, I started to discover who I was. I asked myself what made me angry and what made me happy. I made a list of the people I felt angry or disappointed with and looked at the outcome of each situation, and how I had acted. None of the results were very positive. I realised that I had unrealistic expectations of myself and everyone else. I expected those around me to help me carry the burden or give me the answers, and when this didn't happen I had even more disappointment. I was constantly tired and not feeling motivated or happy and spent a lot of time by myself. I read everything I could find on spiritual growth, and attended every course I could find on healing the mind, body and spirit. I attended and held fire-walks, sweat-lodges, reiki, meditation and motivational seminars. I was committed to the life long search to understand why I felt how I did.

My whole life seemed to come to a crisis point in 1999 when I was in a near fatal car accident. I was trapped in the car for five hours in a river in extremely cold conditions. I decided in that moment that it was probably much easier to just give up on life and then I would not have any worries at all. The ambulance driver had other ideas about my survival; he did everything in his power to keep me alive. The interesting thing is that my body was completely broken on the inside but there was no blood anywhere. As they tried to cut me out of the car I kept thinking this must be a dream because there should be blood on my body; I need to wake up and this will all go away. The fact that I could not move any part of my body reinforced this in my mind. It took twelve months to heal my broken body enough to start living a basic life. I knew my life would never be the same again and I realised my spirit was also broken. I surrendered myself to whatever would be. I gave up resisting and fighting to have the life I believed I needed; my whole belief system came crashing down on me.

Over the next twelve months it was as though every negative aspect of my life haunted me. I was angry with the world, I couldn't understand how this could happen to me. Wasn't I a good person doing spiritual work to help people? And if you do good things, you create good Karma so bad things shouldn't happen. If this was true, how could God and my Angels let this happen? Every negative emotion that was ever invented expressed itself through me. My image in the mirror reflected every negative disappointment that represented my life. The loss of my father, my mother being sick, my marriage and relationship failures and everything else that I could think of came to me as frustration and anger. This was the worst experience of my life. I felt helpless. This pain was worse than all the broken bones in my body because it affected my soul and its journey and everything I had believed in.

My spirit was broken and I had no idea how to fix it. I had spent my whole life looking after everyone else, I didn't know how to truly cherish myself. I didn't realise that I had been broken most of my life. It's like little pieces of my heart and spirit had been stolen as I travelled through life, existing in a world that had been created for me by parents, teachers, family, friends and everyone else I had met along the way.

I had changed myself to conform with everyone else's expectations, giving up on my dreams and sense of self to keep everyone happy and to kill the guilt of being different.

As I learnt and grew, I let go of the expectations, I started to peel away the layers and found myself as a raw template of my own creation. I reinvented myself and the anger disappeared. I forgave myself for not being the person everyone expected me to be, and the person I thought they wanted me to be, and started being myself. I decided it was ok for me to be different. I had gifts and abilities that were unique and special. These gifts had kept me separate from everyone else my whole life and made me feel like an outcast. I was always afraid that I would go over the edge and finish up sick like my mother who was classified as mentally ill.

I stopped worrying about what other people thought of me, stopped trying to always do the right thing and stopped trying to make other people happy. I broke all agreements I had made with myself about who I thought I needed to be and started to say no, this is not how I want my life to be. This is not how I want to feel about myself. This is not how the story ends. I need more than just sugar coating, I need to see this life through as the best and most powerful person I can be.

As my spirit started to recognise itself as someone who is unique and different I found there was no room for anger. This realisation gave me the opportunity to set standards and boundaries. I started to say NO. As I started to say no to others in a loving way, it was like I was saying yes to myself. No one stopped loving or liking me because I said no.

As my energy transformed and I became aware of the frequency of anger I noticed some of the anger issues with my clients and looked for ways to help them have the same release that I had experienced. I noticed that not all angry people are abusive, sometimes clients come to me and I ask why they are angry and they just look at me with a blank stare. As I look deeper, I see that they are the ones who give themselves to the world, holding their anger deep down inside, never expressing their true feelings or opinion because they are afraid of upsetting or hurting people. They are holding their anger in their body which makes them tired and tense, or covering their emotions with a barrier pretending they are fine, so no one suspects what is really happening in their life. They never express that they are desperately unhappy and insecure. Compensating by always putting others before themselves and then they feel resentment because they are not fulfilling their own dream or passion. There are all different sorts of angry people. Most anger is based on FEAR. The fear creates the anger which in turn creates the victim, the worst sort of angry person. The victim must always have someone to blame for their pain.

There can never be true success if there is anger. The secret to anger is to know that you are only EVER angry with YOURSELF. You may not feel this is true, but if you look at the last time you were angry it will be very clear that you became angry because the person or persons you were dealing with either didn't do what you wanted them to do and you didn't get your own way. It's a natural and human reaction to blame the rest of the world for your own short comings. A great exercise for this is to buy a note book and call it your upset and anger book. Every time you are upset or angry write down the story behind the reaction and the picture will become very clear about why you are upset. When someone around you is upset or angry, realise they are not upset or angry with you, THEY ARE UPSET WITH THEMSELF. So maybe look at their life and try to figure out why they are upset. This will help you to not take on their issues and may also help them to communicate why they are having a hard time.

I look back at this experience and wonder why I needed to go through it, then I remember the masses of people I have helped in some way, because I decided to move through and believe in never giving up. My experience, as I turned it into an adventure of transformation and learning, created a positive outcome for myself and countless others.

EVERYONE MAKES BAD DECISIONS WHEN THE ARE ANGRY OR UPSET, EVEN THE MOST POWERFUL AND SUCCESSFUL PEOPLE.

THE SEVEN STEPS TO ANGER

1. The incident
2. The reaction
3. The projection
4. The emotion
5. The guilt
6. The physical act
7. The result

Most anger starts with a thought which then turns into words then actions. Language is the communication code for understanding between humans. Once we are taught we are then living in that society and belief. When you were small you had your own perceptions which were rationalised by our parents, teachers etc. You were told you could not, you were not able to, you didn't know how, you will not. Anger, upset, manipulation, control and revenge are all about energy and this energy is reflected in your Aura. If you are suppressing or projecting your anger instead of processing, releasing and healing your pain, you will never feel complete or find inner peace and will always be looking for something to fill the empty void. Some of you will use material goods, work, drugs, alcohol, sport, while others will go from one healer to another.

You are the only person who can create your own healing. You will need guidance, help or information on some sort of practitioner because it is extremely difficult to do it by yourself; the commitment to transform must be yours. Trust that you can find your own unique path to heal your life. You will need to trust that you can be loved for who you are, not for what you give, do, or believe about yourself in the eyes of someone else. You do not need to surrender your soul to be loved unconditionally by anyone. The secret is to love yourself first. Step back and let the other people in your life come to you, lovingly accepting you exactly how you present your true self to them. To love yourself first is to be free of frustration, and fear of loss. Fear of loss creates the need to control. The inability to control leads to fear and anger and then causes upsets. The other person will conform to your new clear frequency or they will leave.

My favourite saying: If there are two Chinese people living in China, eating Chinese food, living in a Chinese house, they treat each other like Chinese people. If the Martian's come down and change one of those Chinese into an Australian, the other Chinese person can no longer treat them the same because they are a different person. It only takes one person to transform in any given situation and everything will be different.

I often talk to people who are stuck in an old relationship and wonder why, when all they do is talk about their ex-partner and blame them for everything. Making your ex-partner wrong, being angry with them because they won't do what you want them to do proves you are angry with yourself. My advice is to sort yourself out and let go of being the victim. There is no rule that I know of that says a partner, present or past, needs to conform or do as they are told. We have freedom of choice. There is no positive outcome if there is anger and a need to control. If your partner doesn't love you anymore, instead of blaming them, find the reason behind your anger and create a space to let your soul have freedom and expression. Heal your life, then you probably won't want that partner anymore and you will find someone on the same frequency as yourself, creating a new exciting chapter in your life. Forgive yourself for not being the person they wanted you to be. You cannot be that person and be happy, you must be true to yourself. How many times do we see someone we know fall in love then suddenly they change, sometimes it's for the better, but mostly it's to please the person they meet because they assume that is what the other person wants. They forget that who they were in the first place is what created the attraction. Lots of my clients come to me with relationship issues. Sometimes they just need to forgive, forget and move on and have a good look at the positive learning they have experienced from the ex-partner and to look at the personal growth and transformation that has been experienced because of the connection. When you stay stuck in the past you become stuck in the hurt, you stay the victim of your own perception of your past story. This makes you become the victim of everyone and everything and that justifies you sabotaging every positive thing in your life.

Sometimes you just need to let go, forgive yourself for not trusting what you knew in the first place and move on. Then make a commitment to heal your broken heart. The true healing must begin with your loss which could have been at any age and for any reason. Maybe your father left or passed away, or you moved schools or towns, maybe it was your first true love; only you know the first broken heart experience, after all, it's your heart. These are some of the most common reasons I have found for broken hearts: divorce of parents, changing towns/schools, losing a pet, loss of grandparents, and being cheated on by the first true love. I have discovered over the years that people use drugs and alcohol as a tool to kill emotional pain. It works maybe once or twice then the brain sorts it all out and makes the pain seem more than it is, so there is a need for more frequent use and stronger drugs. Sometimes this leads to the end of the pain altogether, death. Drug addicts don't take drugs to ruin their life, they use them to kill the pain of loss and failure. Most drug addicts and alcoholics are angry people.

ANGER AND FAMILY

The experience of anger with children is an interesting example. You get angry with your children because they don't do or behave how you tell and expect them to. Children don't understand anger of grownups. They have clear, easy going beliefs that work well for them until you tell them they are wrong, then they in turn react and copy you or become rebellious and angry in return. You come home after a day of frustration and upset, worrying about money, work, not feeling great and immediately reflect it onto your family. Women are the most powerful examples of this. Everyone knows that if mum is happy, it's a happy home. Even if dad arrives home grumpy she can usually keep the home stable and bring dad around by dinner time by just talking to him and being in his presence. If she does the opposite and reacts to his mood, then the whole environment is a mess. If mum comes home from a hard day in a terrible mood, then watch out because nothing is going to be able to create happiness and harmony. Even worse, if she has a call from someone and is happy and friendly on the phone but returns to the angry state of mind when she hangs up, everyone in the room will feel they have done something wrong to upset her or that she loves the other person more than them because the other person makes her happy. This can also work with the father and his actions. A lot of adults blame their parents for their failed lives and how they were treated instead of taking responsibility for themselves. Once you step back and take a very hard look at yourself you will realise, there is only one reason your life is how it is. That is because you created it yourself based on your beliefs about yourself, parents, teachers, friends etc. As you were thinking negative thoughts that is what you created as your reality.

Children usually punish their parents in two ways by failing or by non-communicating. There will usually be one parent they blame for their failures in life. This happens a lot with divorce situations where the angry victimised parent teaches the children to hate the terrible partner who has deserted them and no longer loves them, which is proven and justified by the action of them abandoning their family. Never mind if the leaving partner is dying inside and can no longer exist in that environment. When it comes to anger and revenge the only important element is the pain of the angry person. It can overrule every practical thought and emotion. As the child grows into adulthood they promise they will never be like the parent/parents. Well, guess what happens? You arrive at about 40 years of age and you start to see yourself doing exactly the same as your parent. That really freaks some of you out. What you may need to do is realise that there is a universal law that says we must love and respect our parents and everyone else in the world as humans, but there is no law that says we need to like them. That is our choice. If you don't like someone, why do you judge them or try to change them to fit into your world? Your parents are who they are, not who you want them to be. If you spend the time transforming yourself that you spend expecting or judging others, you would be a much happier person. Don't be angry with your parents because they didn't give you what you thought you wanted; look at the life you have created and the people you have met because you needed to find yourself, move forward and heal.

STEP 1. INNER PEACE EXERCISE

Create your own healing book.

NOW: **Start your journey.**

1. Go back as far as you can into your childhood to present day and pull out the happy memories - write them down. Just express them exactly how they come to you. Find favourite photos, copy them and stick them in your book, write a brief description about the happy event.

2. Beside each event/picture say what you are grateful for.

3. Sit or lie in a comfortable position (in bed before sleep is perfect).

4. Relax and close your eyes.

5. Visualise or remember an event or picture from your book. Keep your eyes closed and feel the happiness. If you could imagine there was a place in your body that you would feel the happy feeling, where do you imagine that place would be? Is it in your heart, legs, throat, head - where would it be?

6. Give the feeling a colour, any colour that comes into your mind. If no colour comes don't worry, just place your hand on your body and feel the happiness and let it spread through your whole body.

7. As you go to sleep let that happy thought be the last thing you think of.

8. Write beside each picture/event where you felt the energy in your body and the colour

9. Do this each day for 21 days.

10. Carry your book with you if you can or keep it beside your bed.

11. Do this exercise every day, even if you feel or see nothing, as it works on a subconscious level.

If you have access to essential oils, healing sprays or essences of any type place a few drops on your hands before you start the meditation process. This will speed up the process and help your spirit to release.

It is a simple exercise designed to gently change the memory in your brain, instead of putting attention on your unhappy past before sleep, it places your attention on being happy and grateful. After all, your unhappy past is only a memory in your mind. Your memory will be the power that runs your life. Everyone has their own story and the level of pain attached to each story is different for everyone.

If you wake up feeling grumpy or tired, remember that the happy memory is replacing the upset memory stored in your body, as a blockage, as it releases it will affect your mood and energy. There must be a release of the old patterns and memories to create a space for new ways of thinking and acting. A little like when you purchase a new lounge, you remove the old one, you don't just dump the new one on top, so why would you do that with your life experiences? This exercise is just a small step. I suggest that you find other modalities and commit to creating the best life you can possibly live.

YOUR AFFIRMATION

"I LOVE MY LIFE, IT IS PERFECT FOR ME,
RIGHT HERE RIGHT NOW, PRESENT TIME
PRESENT PLACE. "

JeanClare

STEP 2. ANGER ACCEPTANCE AND RELEASE EXERCISE

This is a daily affirmation. You can say it for yourself to have self-forgiveness, or think of someone you need to forgive and add their name.

> “I fully and freely forgive. I lose and let go. I let go and let God’s love do it’s perfect work in me, through me, for me. I let go and let God’s love do it’s perfect work in the conscious, subconscious and super conscious activities of my mind, body and affairs. I give thanks that peace, health, plenty and happiness now reign supreme in me and in my world.”
>
> CATHERINE PONDER.

THIS IS WORK FOR YOUR JOURNAL.

1. THE INCIDENT
   Go to the last time you were very upset. Write down the whole situation, even the small details, where you were, who was with you and what happened.

2. THE REACTION
   How did you feel and what were your thoughts? What did the person do, or not do, that made you react?

3. THE PROJECTION
   Who did you direct your anger at? What did you say/do?

4. THE EMOTION
   How did you feel mentally, physically and emotionally? Was it a feeling of being unloved, stupid, unheard, responsible, ignored or some other way of feeling?

5. THE GUILT
   What did you do to make yourself feel better for your bad behaviour? Did you eat chocolate, drink alcohol, buy a present or do something nice for the person you abused, or did you just go quietly silent and withdrawn, cutting off all emotions and feelings, or did you justify your anger in your thoughts by thinking negative thoughts about someone else?

6. THE PHYSICAL ACT
   What is your physically angry act? Do you slam doors, stomp around, yell loudly, hold your body tight and erect, work it off at the gym? You know what you do, so be honest with yourself.

7. THE RESULT
   Write down the result. What did you GET from being angry? Did you get attention, upset someone who didn't play your game, get out of doing something (children are great at this trick), avoid being confronted by deflecting the attention onto someone or something else? What did you get out of acting upset or angry? How do you feel when you yell and swear at someone, or give them the silent treatment, just to get your own way? What do you avoid?

Another beautiful person I met in Los Angeles was Eva Longoria. I was staying with one of my favourite clients - I will call him Mr. D. He was looking at real estate in Beverly Hills. He already had a beautiful home but was looking for a change. The agent called with a property he might be interested in, so we decided to have a look. I had invited my sister to come on this trip because Miranda had given me tickets to the Victoria Secret Fashion Parade and I knew my sister would love the experience. We arrived at the property which was on the market. The only other person there beside the agent was Eva Longoria and her people. As the agent introduced us, it was evident that not only was Eva very beautiful on the outside, she was also beautiful on the inside. She was so dignified and elegant in a casual way that made everyone feel comfortable. We chatted about Australia a little and she charmed everyone there with her gentleness and her smile. Her presence was clear, calm, happy and shining. She was like a beautiful shiny light with a smile. She looked straight at my face, took my hand and smiled, there was no judgement on how we were dressed or who we were. Three effective ways to tell if a person is angry is by their smile and/or their eyes and the body. Happy people have shiny, clear eyes and a ready, genuine smile and a soft, fluid body. Angry people have heavy eyes, sometimes clouded by alcohol or drugs, they don't smile very much and their body is rigid and stressed. They spend a lot of time and energy just keeping themselves together emotionally and mentally; that's why they are often tired, which makes them even more angry.

Anger = disgust, loathing, rage, aggressiveness, boredom and contempt.

Joy = ecstasy, serenity, trust, love, admiration, optimism and happiness.

One of the realities that may help you to create grace and dignity is to remember that other people don't usually think about you what YOU think they think. The negative thought process is in your own mind. You may think someone is angry or upset with you but they are not. You may think others think you are stupid or naive or whatever but they do not. Those thoughts are your projections based on your own past experiences and self-judgements. Miranda Kerr thinks positive thoughts because she believes in herself and has a clear mind. She doesn't dwell on things, but takes one step at a time to resolve any uncertainty she may have about work/life. She is not a reactive person because she knows it's a waste of energy and there are other amazing possibilities she can create with that same energy.

"AS ANGELS HEAL MY HEART,
I EMBRACE THE JOY OF LIVING."

JeanClare

This is a short testimonial from two of my favourite people, Philippa and Patrick, who certainly live their life with grace and dignity.

Hi Jeannie,

I was so happy to hear that your book 'Never Give Up' is soon to be released. I would like to thank you so much for your guidance and reading last October. Your reading gave me clarity in identifying my emotional blocks and support in giving me the tools to clear these blocks. The Reiki course was a fantastic way to make huge improvements in my life and helped me to assist so many of my friends and relatives. I now feel I am free of the pain that had prevented me from living a fulfilling life. I now have so much to look forward to and have found gratitude in the simple things in life. You have also helped my son Patrick, as he has had the motivation to build on and improve his knowledge in his chosen profession and is forging ahead. We both talk about you often and reflect upon our readings to help us to enrich our lives. We both wish you the very best of luck with your book - I know we will certainly be interested in purchasing it when it is released.

You are a very special person and we feel blessed to have met you. Thank you again.

Much love

Philippa & Patrick Horvath

Chapter 2

COURAGE

Yael Lilienfeld

Chapter 2

COURAGE

Yael Lilienfeld

"Never give up on your dreams, keep following your passion and let yourself be guided by your heart combined with your intuition (gut feeling)."

"That's the way I try to live my life since I was a little girl. I recall visiting NYC for the first time as a young child with my parents. I was probably around 7 years old. NYC and its unique energy fascinated me right away. A city that feels alive! On one hand it seemed to give a lot of energy and on the other hand it seemed to take a lot, but what fascinated me the most was its fast paced energy. A city full of doers and shakers. A city that seems to never sleep. A city where dreams can be turned into reality.

Born and raised in Switzerland I have never experienced something like this before. I sensed, during this very first NYC visit, that one day I would somehow go back to this fascinating city. I guess thinking about my first NYC trip now I must have created, consciously and unconsciously, one of my first dreams right there: Returning one day to NYC and chase some of my yet undefined dreams. It was something I felt deep inside my heart and soul. At that time I had no idea it would turn into reality one day. My brain created a clear imaginary vision of seeing myself breathing and living in the middle of this never sleeping city one day. It felt important to me somehow.

Many years later, after finishing my high school degree in economics and law, I decided it was time to travel and see and experience the world on my own. I made a conscious decision that everything from now on I will learn and teach myself by living, and whatever else I need to learn I will find the answers by reading books and the internet.

Off I was travelling into the unknown, one suitcase, and myself, starting this new chapter. After receiving my high school degree, I supported myself through modelling. I spent some time living and working in Germany, Spain, Greece and France before my path took me finally back to NYC. "Dreams are here to turn into reality."

Here I was about to finally board the plane to NYC. A suitcase in one hand and an open return ticket in the other with no real plan in my mind yet a clear dream of finally returning back to NYC.

It wasn't always easy living and working in NYC. Yet I made a conscious decision that I will always try my best to make it look easy and see in the less positive experiences, the good and turn everything into something positive, no matter what. Frankly living and working in NYC, all on my own at this young age and far away from my family and old friends, was often very challenging on many levels. And during one of those challenging times one of my best girlfriends connected me to Jeannie Moran. At that time I was in a relationship that I felt I needed to end and move on but somehow didn't know how since I was in love with that person. But I knew staying in this relationship would not make us truly happy at the end. I felt this relationship was holding me back. I felt I couldn't "see" clearly anymore. I felt I wasn't able to "hear" my heart and intuition anymore. I felt like I was stuck. During that time I started talking to Jeannie over some phone sessions. She gave me wonderful guidance and shared with me some of her knowledge and I was able to leave my boyfriend and learn to listen to my own heart, passion and intuition again to continue going after my dreams.

And that's what I have been doing ever since.

Over the past few years I turned one of my passions into reality and started my first patented jewellery piece called 'Precious Secrets.' It felt important to create a meaningful jewellery piece that connects people with each other and brings additional happiness into people's life.

I am a strong believer in whatever you do in your life, do it with passion from your heart and listen to your own intuition. Your intuition has the power to guide you on the way to turning those dreams into reality. Keep believing and going after your dreams because one day those dreams will be reality. Don't be scared. And in those moments when you need a solution to something, just sit quietly and ask the universe to assist you in somehow revealing the solution to you. Let go and trust this process. And somehow the answers to the solution will come or be shown to you in the most fascinating and unexpected ways. Magic does exist, you just need to believe in its power. It always worked with me. No one said it would always be easy to keep staying true to your passion, heart and intuition but what I can promise you is it will be worth the ride and you will be rewarded in a very meaningful way. You will enjoy what you do and this will add happiness to your daily life. I feel this world could be in such a better place if we all would follow our heart and passion on a daily basis. It all starts within. If we are happy with what we do and who we are we will spread this positive and happy energy around and hopefully inspire others to start following their passion, heart and dreams too. In my opinion, this could add to a happier and more peaceful planet.

I will forever be thankful for the wonderful guidance and knowledge Jeannie shared with me. She inspired me to keep walking my path and continue chasing my dreams and hopefully on the way I am inspiring others to do the same."

As I wrote many years ago:

> "Whatever comes from your heart will end up inside other hearts."
>
> YAEL ~ WWW.YAELJEWELRY.COM

Yael Lilienfeld

Yael Lilienfeld is one of the most courageous people I have ever met. She is such a gentle soul with such a fine bone structure that she can give the impression of being fragile. She radiates a truly beautiful vibration that is matched by her physical beauty. I love spending time with her whenever I can. To move from modelling to creating her jewellery range 'Precious Secrets' must have taken an exceptional amount of courage. Her desire to help humanity and her gentle nature are expressions of her courage. The ability to be open to creative intuition can be one of the hardest things to do. To be able to trust in the process of life and destiny is truly courageous. Yael's self-belief and the need to share her beautiful creations with the world are what makes her find courage to never give up.

To have courage is special, it's something we don't think about unless we hear or see someone who has been courageous in the news by saving someone in danger. I think we need to see this character trait in ourselves a lot more so we can appreciate how special we are for just breathing and walking. Everyday lots of people out there find mammoth amounts of courage to just get out of bed. The thought of being courageous evokes thoughts of great deeds and heroes of soldiers charging up a hill to destroy the enemy or a fireman rushing into a burning building. I guess there are all different kinds of courage, sometimes we find courage in the strangest times and places, some of those times are in our darkest thoughts, our broken heart, our need to survive or even to forgive. Regardless of where it comes from we all have courage, we just don't think about it. I often wonder where it comes from. Is it something we inherit from our ancestors or is it a human trait that belongs to everyone? I know that belief and passion help create it and help it to grow. One of the strongest emotions connected to courage I believe is love.

When things go wrong as they sometimes will,
When the road you're trudging seems all uphill,
When the funds are low and the debts are high,
And you want to smile but you have to sigh,
When care is pressing you down a bit
Rest if you must, but don't you quit.
Success is failure turned inside out,
The silver tint on the clouds of doubt,
And you can never tell how close you are,
It may be near when it seems afar.
So, stick to the fight when you're hardest hit
It's when things go wrong that you mustn't quit.

UNKNOWN

I think it takes a lot of courage to create clear communication. To sit with someone you care about and be truthful with them in a loving way about anything, I think takes more courage than jumping into a burning building. Don't get me wrong, those people who risk their lives are heroes but I think they are a special breed of humans who have the protector mechanism built into their DNA and I think it's a different sort of courage. To speak the truth about who you are takes a lot of courage, the fear of losing someone you love because you speak your truth can create a lot of fear. Lots of people live in a lie because of it. Becoming someone else in a relationship to please your partner is sometimes easier than being true to yourself and trusting that the other person loves you for who you are. Faith and trust are tested when we are courageous.

I wonder how the world would be if we didn't take away the courage of children, if we didn't ask them for the truth and then punish them because they own up to the deed, or if when they put their hand up in class to answer a question and were praised for trying to answer instead of being told they are wrong. When they are noisy and happy we tell them to be quiet, when they talk to imaginary friends we tell them it's not real, we tell them they can't wear odd socks or a fairy dress to the shops. I wonder what decision they would make about themselves if they were encouraged and not discouraged.

As we live in our relationships we have nothing to compare our life with except our past experiences. If the new relationship is an improvement on the last one then we tend to stay, but what often happens is that we slip back into past behaviour and recreate the same old way of living. Recreating the experience of sadness, lack of motivation and upset, we often stay because of fear of the perception of another failure by our family and friends and the raised eyebrows about another failed relationship and the projected image of the perfect family that is represented by commercial society.

The strange thing about our need to fit into the perfect society is so hypocritical because we make heroes of those individuals who step outside the boundaries. The classic example of this is Apple, and Steve Jobs. I wonder if he ever considered the amount of courage he needed to have to do what he did, or if he just decided it was something he wanted to do and didn't think of the consequences.

It takes a lot of courage to trust in a relationship. Remember when you are having doubts they are yours, not your partners. The physical presence takes away the insecurity that manifests in the mind which reflects how you feel. If your partner is absent physically or emotionally for some reason your mind can play tricks on you by letting you create negative thoughts about what they are doing. The insecurities that you have in thought can be true because they are based on intuition or are they false because they are based on fear. Knowing the difference between fear and intuition only comes from being aware of your own feelings and fears.

KNOWING YOUR SOUL PATH NUMBER MAY HELP YOU UNDERSTAND YOURSELF AND FIND YOUR COURAGE.

To find your soul path number simply add your whole birth date together.

16/07/1987 = 1+6+7+1+9+8+7=39 = 3+9 =12 = 1+2 = 3 - your soul path number is 3

or 1/5/2009 =1+5+2+9=17=1+7= 8 - your soul path number is 8

SOUL PATH NUMBER 1

A number 1 soul person is usually a very singular person, you can spend lots of time by yourself, forgetting about the rest of the world. You can be very intuitive and not even realise it, thinking that everyone else knows what you know. Letting others know what is going on in your life is often unimportant and can cause disharmony because loved ones don't know where you are or where you are going. Because you know what they are doing and can tune into where they are and know they are safe, you forget that they may not necessarily have the same gift. This goes with employees as well; you will see the big picture or the outcome and become frustrated because others cannot create the same vision. Clear communication is the answer for you, and remember, because you know it, it doesn't mean that everyone else knows what you know. You are the type of person who could go off into the desert with a bottle of water and a loaf of bread and forget to tell anyone, then wonder why they are upset with you. Being different to the norm is usually your key to happiness and success. One of your soul's lessons is to learn its ok to ask for help and to realise you need people. You are very caring and often a humanitarian in your spare time. You usually need your space and can be a very private person. Everyone will love you because you have a way of fitting in with all people and helping them to feel comfortable, born to lead because of your passionate nature, love to win because it's fun and don't usually lust after power. Because of your unique gift of understanding yourself and not needing others, you can sometimes be mistaken for being selfish.

Tom Hanks Birthday 9-7-1956=1

Steve Jobs 24-2-1955=1

Martin Luther King 15-1-1929=1

Napoleon Bonaparte 15-8-1769=1

Luke Gottwald 26-9-1973=1

Spencer Tracey 5-4-1900=1

SOUL PATH NUMBER 2

Number 2 people are busy, every minute of every day they are thinking and/or doing something. You even find it difficult to watch television and not get up or do something else at the same time. You love people but do not suffer fools, and often don't want to go out to meet anyone socially but when you get there you are usually the life of the party. Because you are quick witted and very perceptive you don't understand how other humans cannot see the big picture or what is wrong with the world. Your motto is usually how can people be so stupid and can't they see the outcome of their actions? Because you are extremely intelligent and very charismatic you may have several career paths. Number 2 people can often make excellent teachers and leaders and want to make a positive difference in the world. You love to be loved, but find it hard to forget or forgive those who have wronged you on more than one occasion. Family is always a priority of number 2, you always need to know everyone is safe and happy. You are usually very happy, have lots of friends and are easily liked, even though you can be grumpy sometimes. Your belief is, if I can see or feel it, I can achieve it.

Barack Obama's birthday is 4-8-1961=2

Madonna 16-8-1958=2

Jennifer Lopez 24-7-1969=2

Michelle Obama 17-1-1964 =2

Melina Trump 26-4-1970=2

Tony Robbins 29-2-1960=2

Bill Clinton 19-8-1946

Charles Prince of Wales 14-11-1948

Prince William 21-6-1982

John Glen 18-7-1921

Prince Philip Duke of Edinburgh 10-6-1921

SOUL PATH NUMBER 3

This is the number of the roller coaster; your life seems to be an endless journey of highs and lows. You are very creative and usually have only one passion as a career, although you may do variations of the same career or passion. You can be prone to being a bit down or depressed and need to find ways to pick yourself up and climb back up to the top of the roller coaster. Number 3s can be very addictive because of the low feelings and find it hard to give up addictions or bad habits. You can be stubborn and set in your ways. This can make some relationships difficult. As a number 3 you can become the best in the world at what you do because you are so passionate about your gifts. Lots of love for music and the arts are often part of keeping on top of the hill. It is your journey to learn to maintain balance of the highs and lows so your destiny follows a straight path. You are very loyal and defend your family at any cost but can also not need to be close to family if you are in a negative state of mind. You can at times lack strength in your convictions because of your lack of self-belief and rely on others to provide you with success.

Hillary Clintons birthday is 26-10-1947 which is a number 3. This number reflects her roller coaster career and marriage.

Kylie Minogue has a birthday on 28-5-1968. Number 3 reflects her roller coaster health and relationships.

Judy Garland 10-6-1922=3

Audrey Hepburn 4-5-1929=3

SOUL PATH NUMBER 4

Soul path 4 is very interesting. Very intelligent and usually having an excellent memory, you categorise everything in your mind like a filing system. Everything is in boxes with labels and that's how your mind works. When you are working, you wear your work hat, when you are playing you wear your play hat. While you do this, nothing else is on the radar screen, everything is connected to what you are doing at any given time. Number 4s are usually the most loyal of all humans. You are not flexible in your thoughts and can be set in your opinions and ways, seeing only one way to do things. In your world, you are either happy or sad, it's sunny or it's raining, there are no grey areas. You make excellent law enforcement, accountants, lawyers, judges and soldiers, any career that requires balance you will love. You are a very good friend and care about family, find it hard to forget, and easy to forgive. You can be hard on yourself and others at times because you are a little bit of a perfectionist. Your life path journey is to learn to be a little more flexible and a little less judgemental. Friends will love being around you and visiting you at home because you are sincere in your actions and friendship. You are usually great at saving money and extremely good at business. You always like to win and often don't listen to the advice of others, sometimes too stubborn for your own good and need to be careful about addictive behaviour.

Donald Trump's birthday is 14-6-1946=4

King Henry 8th 28-6-1491=4

Russell Crowe's birthday is 7-4-1964=4

SOUL PATH NUMBER 5

As a number 5 you are very multi-talented and may have many different and varied careers. Some of you will eventually realise why you have learnt about so many different modalities and bring them all together to create an amazing business or career from the best of what you have learnt. 5s love and need people but don't always like them. You make a great sales person because you will always think of how the other person feels. You can be impulsive and need to learn about money and how to save money. Any career where you deal with people is excellent for a number 5 because you can be reclusive at times. I always think of number 5 soul path angels as having ants in their pants because they can't sit still. Usually very creative and having a vision for the future, number 5s are romantic dreamers and are often misunderstood because they can't always show their emotions if anyone else is around. You will go to a quiet place and be upset or angry by yourself. If you do erupt with someone, it's like Mount Vesuvius exploding. You readily forgive but never forget and once you cut someone off, that's it, you will never be in their life again. You often turn to nature or children to save. Number 5's are the doers and can be impulsive. Your life lesson is to stay focused on the big picture and not go off chasing butterflies and other non-realistic dreams.

Vincent Van Gough 30-3-1853=5

Zoe Saldana 19-6-1978=5

Louis Armstrong 4-8-1901=5

Bette Midler 1-12-1945=5

Abraham Lincoln 12-2-1809=5

SOUL PATH NUMBER 6

Number 6 souls are mostly quiet achievers, you have a lot of thoughts moving around in your brain, and need to figure everything out and make it simple. Your life lesson is to trust yourself and to find your voice and speak up about what you believe in. Emotional communication can be very difficult and you will tend to do physical things to show how you feel instead of expressing your emotions through communication. You can easily spend time by yourself and dislike being bossed around. You respond to loving persuasion and are not usually aggressive. You can be very loyal and don't need lots of friends or a big social life if you are in a happy relationship or career. Number 6 souls are the glue that holds the universe together. Number 6s are very deep and sometimes keep lots of secrets, you know things but often don't talk about it because you fear people will think you are strange. You can be deeply spiritual and have a strong connection to the stars and the universe.

Albert Einstein 14-3-1879=6

Thomas Edison 11-2-1847=6

SOUL PATH NUMBER 7

Soul path 7s are the fallen Angels. You are extremely sensitive, often avoid people and can take ages to find your passion. You are here to learn compassion firstly for yourself and then for humanity. You can be addictive by nature, using your addiction to avoid life and your purpose. Usually gentle by nature, but have a very strong disposition which allows emotional balance except when angry. You can forget but never forgive. Your friends will need to be true and forgiving because you can tend to forget about them when you are busy. You are usually very creative and love to combine this talent with your career. You have the ability to be able to create great change in the world if you follow your heart and not your head. Extremely gifted you have a special connection to the almighty, you just need to believe in what you can't see and in yourself. If you decide to work to help humanity it will give you a feeling of inner peace. This can be difficult because you like to be behind the scenes so you don't have to deal with people. You love a simple, relaxed life style with a hint of adventure. Being very good at saving money and generous by nature, you will readily give to those less fortunate.

Buzz Aldrin 20-1-1930=7

Johnny Depp 9-6-1963 =7

Diana Princess of Wales 1-7-1961=7

Queen Elizabeth II 21-4-1926=7

SOUL PATH NUMBER 8

You are the physical leaders of the world, good at business and making money or marrying someone who has money. Because you represent the physical element of the universe, you need to be physically present to make your money. Balance and harmony are necessary for your success. You can make millions and lose millions because of your obsessive, driven personality. Number 8s are very loyal and make excellent friends. You are born under the sign of infinity and have all gifts and talents to achieve anything you desire, as long as you don't obsess over it. You can carry anger for a long time and find it hard to feel compassion for others less fortunate which makes you an excellent achiever who can see the work that needs to be completed to create a desired outcome. Like a good red wine, you become wiser and happier with age. Your physical presence will be remembered long after you have left this earth.

Barbra Streisand 24-4-1942=8

Nelson Mandela 18-7-1918=8

Elizabeth Taylor 27-2-1932=8

Grace Kelly 12-11-1929=8

SOUL PATH NUMBER NINE

The wisest of all souls, you are very loyal and dependable. Need to finish what you start and to know when to finish what you have started, you can tend to stay too long in a situation and need to listen to your intuition when it tells you to move on. This can often be the last incarnation for you, so experiencing everything while you are still here will be important.

You can be extremely compassionate and believe in humanity despite its faults, ever the dreamer and believer. You will often start projects or courses and not finish them; this is because you have memory from many previous lifetimes and sometimes just need a reminder of how things work. You have all the knowledge and information you need to achieve any dreams or desires in this lifetime, just make sure you don't allow yourself to be responsible for other people's dreams. It's important to complete your dreams as you may not come back. You will often enter this lifetime free of karma so any karma you have will be self-created.

Mother Teresa 26-8-1910=9

Robert Redford 18-8-1936=9

Miranda Kerr 20-4-1983=9

Your soul path number is yours for life, it belongs to you and is a guide for you to use to help you understand yourself and those around you. The perfect partner can sometimes be the same soul number, as with Barak and Michelle Obama. I have only ever come across a few people who have found the same soul path partner and they have all had wonderful lives together. Remember your personality can also be influenced by your numerology and your star sign, I only use them all as a guide to help me stay on track and to understand myself and to accept that I sometimes do what I do because that's how God made me. I don't allow the information to justify bad behaviour, I use it to create better ways of acting because I accept my negative traits and I know I have a choice about how I treat myself and everyone else.

Chapter 3

TRANSFORMATION

Pete Everett/
John Scott

Chapter 3

TRANSFORMATION

Pete Everett/ John Scott

> God may be the creator of the universe but you are the creator of your own life.

Whether you realise it or not, you have a choice every morning when you get out of bed. You even have a choice about the time you get out of bed. Have you ever wondered why you say in your mind, I will get up at 6am and go running or walking and not do it or use the slightest excuse to avoid living some part of your life to the fullest? It's not because you don't want to achieve your goals, it's because deep inside you are afraid. Maybe everything will change and that could cause a recurrence of emotional pain that you experienced in the past and subconsciously you cannot go through that experience again. If you exercise and look fantastic, you will start to shine and then everyone will notice you and your life will transform. That could be scary on a deep subconscious level. Emotional pain and disappointment are the biggest subconscious saboteurs we have locked in our memory bank.

TRANSFORMATION

Transformation is like a tree standing in the forest surrounded by dead leaves and fallen branches. It sometimes feels the sun or the rain on its leaves and feels happy, and sometimes there is no sun and no rain and it is unsure of its future but it keeps growing and surviving. Then one day there is a tsunami and the tree is flooded, stripped of its leaves and its protective bark. It almost drowns. It will either bend with the flow of water or it will break and be destroyed. When the water recedes, it looks around at the mess and wonders how it can rebuild its life to be better, stronger and more purposeful. This is the beginning of your life. Transformation. Those of you who decide to bend and believe there is light at the end of the tunnel will recreate yourself to be the amazingly clear, vibrant and shiny stars you are meant to be. Those of you who give up will live as you always have, waiting for the next tsunami to destroy your life so you can blame something other than yourself for your life of unfinished dreams and disappointments.

The most profound and life changing tools I have experienced, taught and learnt are:

REIKI, KINESIOLOGY, MEDITATION, YOGA, FLOWER and other ESSENCES, N.L.P, CRYSTALS, SWEATLODGES, FIRE WALKING, PAST LIVES, THEATRE OF THE MIND by Matt Fury and THE DYNAMIC LAWS OF PROSPERITY by Catherine Ponder.

THE SEVEN LEVELS OF TRANSFORMATION

> “To have true transformation, I believe you need to truly know yourself.”
>
> PETE EVERETT

Pete Everett, the television presenter/actor, is a happy, sensitive and gifted personality.

I met Pete several years ago, when I was in one of my ‘I’ve had enough of people’ moods. I was so determined to retire that I moved from my home town of Coffs Harbour to the Gold Coast and hoped that no one would find me. Well someone gave my number to Pete and when he called and I said yes, come and see me, how that happened I still don’t know, but I am so glad it did. He inspired me to not retire and give up on humanity. I felt if there are others out there as aware, sensitive, strong and open to transformation as him, then I will keep working. If I ever feel alone or sad, I think of Pete and immediately I feel a warm glow around my heart. I am sure that when he was born the Angels looked down from heaven and thought he was one sensitive little fellow, so they sent one of their own down to share his life, and make it more interesting. He has knowledge about life and spirituality that is just there when he needs it. This is not an easy path to walk and takes a lot of courage and transformation to believe. I know there are many times in Pete’s life when he could have given up but he didn’t. He trusted the process and came out the other side stronger and clearer than ever.

Sometimes terrible things happen in our lives to make us transform. I believe it is part of our destiny. I know when Pete lost his position as presenter on the show Ready Steady Cook, he was devastated. Not only because he was treated badly, it was also the shock of the whole situation which he had no control over. He may have felt it coming but didn't read the signs as well as he could have. We become complacent and think we are controlling our own destiny. I remember when I had my car accident, I was trying to leave my clairvoyant work behind. I wanted to be normal. I purchased a business franchise. On the way home from setting up the office for the business, I had the car accident. I remember as my then partner took the keys from me (I was meant to be driving) my intuition screamed at me to take the keys back and drive, but I didn't. We were travelling 100kmh in a 40 zone, the bridge had been removed and a detour set up. The driver didn't see the detour and we flew off the road and became airborne. The workmen had left one pylon from the old bridge standing near the far edge of the river, everything else had been removed, but they had trouble getting that one to move so they left it. The car just happened to hook itself on the pylon which stopped it from smashing into the new cement wall on the other side and dropping into the river and being submerged. I remember as we were flying through the air a ball of golden light came through the windscreen and surrounded me. That memory of the ball of light and the last pylon being left there gave me hope that everything was going to be exactly how it was meant to be. The car still smashed into the river bank and was concertinaed and partly submerged but if the pylon had not been left there the results would have been fatal. Like Pete, it wasn't so much the accident that fazed me, it was more how I was treated by the insurance company that madc me completely transform who I was and how I acted and felt.

Some people lose their wealth, some are diagnosed with cancer, some have relationship breakups, some lose a family member - there are lots of different reasons why we decide to transform our lives, trust the process and get ourselves back on the destiny path. The greater force has a position and purpose for each one of us and it will do whatever it needs to make us see the right path. One of the easiest people I have worked with was Zoe Saldana. I was staying in Beverly Hills with a client and he asked me if I would see one of his friends. He mentioned she was a brilliant actress and a beautiful person, but she was a little stuck career wise. I did three sessions with her and was amazed with how quickly she embraced the transformation. There was no holding onto the past, blaming or judging anyone else; she just took everything in her stride with grace and dignity. I remember looking at my notes after she left the first time and was a little shocked because I had advised her to let go of the television series and take other acting opportunities (I often don't remember what I say to someone after a session is finished). She was a little hesitant because I could tell she loved working on the show. But instead of staying in the old way of thinking and acting she stepped into an amazing career and went on to bigger and better things. She is a very down to earth, gentle and caring person who has a pure heart. When you are going through a transformation, it's easy to give up or to be hard on yourself. The easiest way to stay on the path is to sometimes ask yourself what you can do differently to improve your future, what is the most stressful event in my life right now that I need to simplify or resolve? What are some techniques I can use daily or weekly to help clear my mind and stay grounded? What do I need to do for myself that is kind, nurturing and loving, that reflects my feelings of being whole and complete?

Those of you who are on the treadmill of transformation will need to embrace constant change; the transformation allows the spirit to embrace the journey of the soul. There may be a new career, house or even relationship changes that raise eyebrows of those who know you. This will bring back the belief that there is something, different, missing, wrong with you. Being aware that the transformation process requires personal growth, and change will help you to accept yourself. I frequently have some of you come to me and ask about the lesson you needed to learn from a failed relationship or career choice. It is not always about learning a lesson, sometimes it is about moving on and knowing yourself better. Being gentle with yourself and accepting who you are without comparison to the rest of the world will help you to transform. Instead of looking for the lesson, look for the inner growth and the self-empowerment you have created because you needed to move forward and create paths for your true self and your intended destiny. If you look around you at people you know there will be obvious signs about the transformations within their world. Some will never have movement and others will be on a water wheel constantly trying to change and move forward but are stuck in the same rhythm going around in circles. Others will be caught in quicksand struggling for a long time then either sinking or breaking free. The more you struggle and fight against transformation, the harder your life path will be. The need to believe and surrender to yourself is paramount. It is important to stay in present time and to be grounded.

Some of us just can't do transformation, it's too painful. Others are forced into a situation of change or lose everything. Then there are those like John Scott who saw the opportunity to live his life with clarity and truth through transformation. As I have connected to John over the past couple of years I have at times seen my own reflection in his transformation. John's journey has been one of the most interesting, unusual and amazing I have encountered. He has an extraordinary career as an entertainment specialist, film maker and entrepreneur. John lives in Sydney with his two children. He is the founder of the virtual agency, Platform Me, where he takes great pride in nurturing and developing the transformation of people from all over the world.

John Scott

HONOUR & AWARD

In 2005, John was the recipient of a prestigious Lion award at the Advertising and Media awards in Cannes.

In 2006, John wrote and directed a short film, ***HOOKED,*** which has enjoyed Film Festival success both in Australia and internationally. John Scott has worked in the Australian entertainment business for over 25 years, his primary focus has been the marketing and management of motion pictures and recorded music.

Scott's experience has been broad and varied, having marketed some of the biggest motion pictures and musical acts in the world today. Motion pictures which have enjoyed both box office and critical acclaim include – ***Back To The Future; James Bond; Elizabeth, Portrait Of A Lady; Moulin Rouge; Star Wars; X-Men.*** Musical successes include ***U2; and INXS.*** He has managed the image and positioning of the likes of Levis, aussieBum, BVLGARI, Sarah Ferguson Duchess of York, Cate Blanchett, Nicole Kidman, Toni Collette & Hugh Jackman.

2014 saw the launch of Scott's digital start up Platform Me. The world's first fully automated, social media platforming agency.

John Scott lives in Sydney.

Transformation

~ **NOUN** – a marked change in form, nature, or appearance:

"Jean has helped me understand the true meaning of transformation. Over the years that I have had readings from Jean, I have come to understand that, whilst her ability to see and sense things that are on the horizon for me... they mean nothing unless I am open to idea of transformation.

As living, breathing entities on a cellular level, we are transforming every second of every day....this transformation is simply not in our control. Acknowledging transformation on a cognitive level is where the real power lies.

Many humans have an inherent fear of change...they seek and feel great comfort in the status quo. Many people are curious about the idea of transformation as it conjures the idea of change for the better.

Transformation is not about changing the past or the future. Transformation doesn't live in the future, it is very much about how we approach things that are presented to us in real time. True transformation is about accepting and acknowledging that nothing lasts forever and that everything changes continuously.

Like every single person on the earth, I have continually transformed. I have had life altering experiences with life altering outcomes. I have had enduring relationships with people whom contributed to my transformation. I have loved deeply and I have had the gift of being loved in return.

Through Jean's masterful gift, I have come to learn that every single opportunity that presents itself, every incident that happens, people that we meet, have all contributed to the continual transformation of us as human beings.

Like all humans, I have a story. There have been great highs and very low, lows. I have experienced the great gift of parenthood, I have had the wonder of loving a human being who loves you back. That gift was only countered by the devastating loss of holding that person in my arms as she passed away, all too early. I have embarked on a relationship with a beautiful man who taught me that love is not about gender...at the risk of sounding fatalistic, he also confirmed for me that nothing lasts forever. I have built solid careers and changed them. I have made money and lost money, built businesses and lost businesses. All of these experiences have only added to the continual transformation of me as a human being.

Thank you, Jean, for your wonderful insight into human behaviour, for encouraging me to believe that our life experiences are the gifts that ensure that we continually grow and learn as individuals. This is transformation."

John Scott

www.platformme.me

> “Self-transformation is not just about changing yourself. It means shifting yourself to a completely new dimension of experience and perception.”
>
> JAGGI VASUDEV

To have transformation, there needs to be trust. To have trust, there needs to be a balance between INTELLIGENCE AND INTUITION. If you have a war going on in your head between your intuition and your intelligence there is no way you will be able to trust yourself. You will talk yourself out of clarity into confusion. How many times have you said to yourself I need to…….and not followed through, only to find that if you had, your day, week would have been much easier? When you were little your intuition was happy, you skipped, sang, coloured in pictures how you wanted to, wore your clothes inside out and back to front and didn't care. As you grew older your intelligence was trained by society and you started to let it run your life. How many times have you gone out with someone or applied for a work position knowing you were wasting your time and did it anyway? Your intelligence has told you that you needed to do those things because if you didn't you would probably miss out and there may not be another chance. Your intuition would have told you to be patient, the right thing will come along, trust and believe in yourself. I love lists but sometimes they are not positive for us to have. When you write your list, it is a commitment to do whatever is written down and if you don't complete each action you get upset or annoyed with yourself and your intelligence gives you a hard time about it or tells you not to worry it wasn't important to do the things allocated anyway.

MY COMPLETED DAY DIARY

Most of the time we only look at what we haven't achieved, not what we have.

One of the most empowering things I have discovered is to have two diaries. This happened by accident, someone special to me gave me a diary and I had already purchased one for myself. I loved the one given to me and didn't want to waste it. Let's face it, you only have one year to use a diary. I started to use both. My everyday diary I used as normal, appointments, shopping etc.

My second diary I used in a different way. This is how it happened. I was having a very bad day, giving myself a hard time because the tasks in my everyday diary were not complete. I hadn't completed even half the list. I made a coffee, sat on my lounge and thought about the day and where it had disappeared to. I looked up and saw my second diary sitting unused on the coffee table and a little voice in my head said, why don't you use that diary to write down everything you did do today? My brain was a little resistant to say the least, but my body moved on its own accord and picked up the diary. I opened the page at the relevant date and wrote down everything I could remember doing that day. Starting from getting out of bed, having breakfast, cleaning teeth, having a shower, checking emails, answering emails, doing the dishes, everything I could think of I wrote down from the minute I woke until I went to sleep that night. When I finished, I looked at the list and was astounded and so was my brain. I wondered how I had ever found the time and energy to achieve so much in one day. I DID THIS PROCESS FOR 30 DAYS and I felt amazing. I found not only did I complete my need to do the list but

I accomplished so much more. If I have a day now where I start to give myself a hard time I just write a complete day list and it seems to stop the negative words in my mind and turns them into self-praise. It also made me look at how much time I wasted on the phone talking about irrelevant things to people who were just wasting my time, it also made me very aware of which friends I was spending time with who only focused on themselves, and those who were productive and positive. The big realisation was how much time I wasted on social media, looking at emails from companies selling things that I wasn't even interested in, like lottery tickets for houses, seminars in America, holidays and heaps more. I unsubscribed from everything I knew I didn't need. Let's face it, you only need to google holiday destinations and a million sites come up, this is far less time consuming than checking weekly emails.

MY COMPLETED DAY

This diary must be a real book. I believe that cyber space books do not work as you cannot feel or touch them, so your brain will not register them as a true object because they don't truly exist.

Do this exercise just once and you will be amazed! To have a shift in brain patterns you will need to commit to doing this process for 7 or 30 days.

Woke up

Made breakfast and the beds

Packed everyone's lunch

Took children to school

Bough fuel for the car

Made a coffee - took 5 mins to sit and enjoy it

Did the laundry

Tidied the kitchen

Made appointments for clients and sorted my diary for the week

Talked to Mary for 30 mins

Checked emails, Facebook and Instagram

Answered 10 emails

List everything

Ok now you have your day listed.

How long is the list? How amazing has your day been and how much have you achieved? The thing you have forgotten in your need to be perfect is how much you do achieve in your day/life. **Every time you make a list of things to do, that list is subconsciously in your head taking up space, time and energy. LIKE A DVD when you empty that space IT CREATES THE OPPORTUNITY TO OPEN NEW LISTS and allows your brain to rest and feel completed. Whenever you have things on your lists uncompleted, it will sit in your subconscious and cause negative thoughts.** You know it feels empowering to complete tasks that have been on your mind for a long time, especially when you keep saying to yourself I should do such and such. De-clog your brain and take the stress away by using your COMPLETED list as motivation. You will be surprised how much extra time and energy you have and how happy and proud you feel when you look at your completed list every day. You may also apply this to people in your past that are still in your mind taking up space and energy. Complete it with them, sit down and write a letter and say you are sorry you can't be the person they want you to be, write down all the things you are grateful for about them and give it to them or burn it. Don't let someone from your past be more important in your thoughts than yourself.

To have integrity is about keeping your word. If you say even to yourself that you will do something you need to do it, no matter how small it is. If you tell your child you will take them somewhere or do something, you need to do it, or if you can't let them know why you can't and make other arrangements. If you break your word it hurts two people, you and the other person. This also applies when you promise yourself something and then give that time and energy to someone else. It disempowers you and you will feel resentment because you are doing for someone else.

WHAT YOU DECIDED ABOUT YOURSELF

One of the major keys for transformation is to understand the decision you have made about yourself because of another person's actions. This will be a reasoning you create because of other people, not a conscious thought you make about yourself. It will be something that you experienced when you were young. Probably between the age of 4 and 8. Probably something simple, disappointing but not necessarily traumatic. You can visit a practitioner to find out what it is, but it's just as easy to do it yourself. My example is, I remember when I was about 6 or 7 years old I went to school one day excited to spend time with my best friend whom I loved dearly. I looked for her in the playground and in class, but she wasn't there. When I asked the teacher why she wasn't at school I was told that the family had moved away and I wouldn't see her again. I was confused, I couldn't understand why she hadn't told me they were moving and why didn't she say goodbye. When I looked at the situation I realised I had made a decision, THERE MUST BE SOMETHING WRONG WITH ME, and that's why she didn't say goodbye. I have compounded that decision in every relationship or friendship I have ever experienced, even with my family. Quite often when I say things to family they look at me as if I come from another planet or just ignore the conversation and I take it that there is something wrong with me, then I turn it around and realise that I know things that they don't. My career also didn't help, seeing people who have passed over, having visions of the future, being able to scan a person's body for health issues are all talents that reinforce that I'm different and that there is something wrong with me. I also believe that was the moment I decided to develop my intuition so I would know if that was going to happen again in my future.

To find your decision you can try the following. Remember this is not about what is holding you back or preventing your success etc., it's about your decision about you that separates you from other people.

1. Find a quiet place to lay or sit, close your eyes and relax.

2. Go to the first sad memory you remember, it may not be traumatic or heartbreaking, it's just something that made you sad.

3. Think about what happened, focus on the other person or whatever else is present besides yourself. It may be a pet or a person.

4. Look at what happened, like it's a little story or movie running in your head.

5. Reflect on how you felt emotionally.

6. Look for other times you have felt like this.

7. Write down every incident you can remember and what happened.

8. Find the common emotion so you can understand the decision that you made about yourself.

It could be:

I'm different to everyone else.

There's something wrong with me.

I don't understand myself (my life, my family, my feelings).

There's something not right (with me, about me, about my life).

There's something missing (in me, for me, with my life).

You may find your decision straight away without needing to do the exercise.

It's important to find someone to help with the healing process with this. I found NLP or hypnotherapy the quickest and most powerful.

Look at how that decision has impacted your relationships with other people.

9. Find the positive side of your decision.

Which will be:

> I allow myself to be different, I feel things other people don't.
>
> I allow myself to be powerful, I see things other people don't.
>
> I allow myself to be special, I hear things other people don't.
>
> I allow myself to be complete, I know things other people don't.
>
> I allow myself to be unique, I think things other people don't.

When you know your belief, you have the key to create a different way of being.

REMEMBER FOR EVERY ACTION, THERE IS AN EQUAL AND OPPOSITE REACTION.

NEWTONS LAW OF MOTION

For every negative action, there is a positive reaction.

For every negative thought, there is positive thought.

For every negative conversation, there are positive words spoken.

For every negative feeling, there is a positive feeling.

When you believe there is something wrong with you, there will be a tendency to feel that emotion every time someone indicates that you are not perfect. Believing there is something wrong or missing with you will attract people who treat you that way, which impacts and reinforces the belief.

If your relationship is a mess, you will feel that there is something wrong with you because the other person doesn't love you, so you must also be responsible for the situation, justifying your belief that there is something wrong, missing, not right with you. This is one of the games of life that you need to let go of. You need to know and believe there is nothing wrong or missing, you are exactly who you are meant to be in this instant. Find a way to release this belief. I worked with Darren Stevens NLP time line therapy to figure it all out. It took me back to when I was three days old, in my mother's arms, being aware of her physical and emotional pain and taking on the responsibility for her emotions. This decision impacted my life in a big way. It's ok to have belief systems in place about ourselves but we cannot have negative beliefs that are detrimental to our lives in every aspect. It's extremely powerful to realise that you are not the person your belief systems say you are. It's even more empowering to learn that you are not the person that your parents predict that you will be. Once you release the need to prove yourself to others you will find self-empowerment. One of the reasons we love to travel to other countries is because it allows us to feel different, and people of other countries love to treat us that way. It allows us to be ourselves without the fear of being ridiculed or feeling there is something wrong. The environment we are in while travelling is alien so we fit in, feel free and happy to climb mountains or hug a tree and it's all ok because we are tourists. We see people of a different nationality acting different to us and it flicks our 'it's ok to be different' switch, because the whole country is acting differently. We are not the same and it seems to fascinate these other races. The other reality is that you will need to be away from your family to find yourself and work this out, because siblings and parents are the most powerful triggers emotionally for 'there is something wrong with me', after all, are they not the people who have told you your whole life that you are wrong, or that you don't know what is good for you, or that you should do things differently? Even if it is because they love you, it still causes a conflict for you between your intuition and the fact that they know what is right for you and you don't.

TRANSFORMATION IS WHAT ANGELS EAT FOR BREAKFAST.

Chapter 4

COMMITMENT

Jeannine Kaspar

Chapter 4

COMMITMENT

Jeannine Kaspar

"I've always felt I have a gift, a gift to give solace or an empathetic knowing glimpse into the life of a person fighting to survive. It might be a role of a woman struggling to regain control of her life after rehabilitation, or it might be the woman coping with another kind of loss and survival. I just didn't feel I had the clarity to accept my gift and what to do with it. I feel like staying my course, being true to my commitment to myself and my gift has itself been the greatest gift.

With Jean's loving guidance I feel like I have become my most authentic self, owning who I am, my talents, and what I want. I am incredibly indebted to her for this guidance along my journey. Even though I was accomplishing goals in my work I felt like a bottle rocket that needed guidance and a reminder of what's important - staying true to myself and never giving up. I recommit myself every day and its working."

Xoxoxo Jeannine www.jeanninekaspar.com

COMMITMENT

The one thing I have learned from Jeannine is your thoughts impact your levels of commitment to yourself and others more than anything else.

I worked with Jeannine to create a shift within the boundaries of her life.

The one secret Jeannine Kaspar taught me about is commitment. I first spoke to her in 2009 and realised she was committed to her craft as the most important goal in her life. She has the most amazing ability to keep going and never give up even when she sometimes doubts herself and the outcome of her situation. I witnessed amazing resolve and perseverance when Jeannine found her little canine friend who had been abused and left to die. She never gave up on him no matter what the predicted outcome was regarding his survival. She is truly an amazing person, who I have come to love and respect as a daughter. I have always been truthful and sometimes a little too harsh with my words to her but she has never backed down or considered giving up on her acting career or transforming her life. Instead of reacting she will consider my words and draw her own balanced conclusion. She is a stunningly beautiful woman and is committed to taking care of her physical, spiritual and emotional bodies. I spent lots of time in New York and Los Angeles with Jeannine, they have been some of the most interesting and fun times of my life. Together we created a balance in her life around her commitment levels to herself and the other people in her life. As I worked with her, teaching her to stay true to herself and to trust her intuition, I realised my own lack of commitment to my spiritual self. I was asking Jeannine to commit to her own acting and empathic gifts, and realised I had been trying to run away from my gifts of psychic ability my whole life.

Commitment to anything means being aware of and not listening to negative conscious and subconscious thoughts. **Fear is the foundation**

for lack of commitment and giving up. The negative thought patterns create the fear, it's as simple as that. To overcome them and break the pattern you need to change the way you think about your future and your part in it. Don't let your immediate needs push aside your hopes and dreams for a better future. Use your vision board and affirmations to keep you on the path of commitment and success. Commitment is an ongoing process. There are those who commit and never give up, doing whatever they need, to create a desired outcome, sometimes above and beyond the natural ability of the mind or body. A very good example of this is sports people. Then there are those humans who try something for 5 minutes and expect their world to be perfectly transformed and wonder why nothing has worked. Choose the worst area of your life and commit to creating change in that space. Everyone has some part of their life that lacks commitment.

One of the most difficult things in life is to stay committed and focused. The older we get the harder it becomes because past memory interferes with how we feel and think. The voice in our head tells us in no uncertain terms consciously or subconsciously that we don't deserve or can't have the outcome we dream or desire. When we are little and we desire something for our birthday we usually manifest it easily. As we get older the glass walls seem to multiply between our desire and the result. If you are using drugs, alcohol, laziness, procrastination, work situation, or a stale relationship as an excuse for failure then look at that situation and be truthful with yourself. Where do you lack commitment? Remember you only ever fail to have commitment for yourself, you may think you are not committed to your work, partner etc. but it's you who are not committed to your own journey to create happiness, fulfilment and abundance. If you are committed to yourself it will be a reflection in your Aura, others will see that reflection and believe in you.

The best judge of your commitment levels to the world is you. Deep inside you know what you don't do that you have promised yourself that you will do. I have a lot of clients come to me and say they can't find a job, partner life style etc. that they want. Why is it not happening? I give them some simple exercises to do that they wanted to commit to like Yoga, meditation, exercise or even spending time talking to their family and they just can't follow through. They make all the excuses in the world for not committing to their own wellbeing. If you can't commit to yourself, how on earth can you expect anyone else to take you seriously and commit to you? There must be a space where your mind allows you to be the most important person in your own life. To sacrifice yourself and your own needs for others is a waste of time and energy and will only make you tired and unhappy. You need to say to yourself, what is important for me right now, what do I need to do, will I have coffee with Mary who always talks about her problems and leaves me tired and depleted or will I go home and do everything that needs to be done and go for a walk? Ok, if you do all the chores you will feel good about that but in the back of your mind you will have that nagging voice saying you didn't do what you promised yourself you would do. If you go for a walk, you will feel great, come back and tidy up any way. Let's face it, when you are laying in the ground in a box and the man is shovelling dirt on your face, it's a bit late to say I wish I had. I should have.......

Nothing comes from doing nothing.

Start with small steps. If you can't handle the big picture, take one step at a time.

If you would like to lose some weight, you must first decide the amount of weight you want to lose, then comes the food and the changes you need to make, then the exercise, also the input of outsiders like a specific diet or beauty treatments to boost the process, then the time you are going to allow yourself to achieve your goal. Have a structured program, as if you don't your brain will interfere and tell you all sorts of interesting negative things. You know this because in the past you have tried before to achieve certain things and have given up without knowing why. The secret to commitment is NEVER GIVE UP and don't get upset if you fail or give up the first time. When something doesn't work, our brain tends to say I told you so and we then wait until we find our courage to start again with the same project or a new one. The more times you tell yourself you have failed, the more power you give your negative identity. The trick is to convince yourself that it's ok, you just need to step back and rethink the process and try some new steps. Putting your certificates or diplomas in a place where you can see them is a powerful indication for you to keep going. To receive any sort of certificate means you have completed something and it can show you how far you have come since you first started. I don't believe certificates are to show how clever we are or where we have studied, I believe they are to show us how much we have grown and what we are sometimes capable of.

When I decided to take on the vocation of clairvoyant, I decided I needed to have complete commitment to myself, my clients and my craft. Every day I would need to work on improving my clairvoyant ability and my sense of self. I knew that people would come to me because they needed help and guidance. I was totally committed to finding out about every healing modality on the planet. I also went and saw every clairvoyant and psychic I could find. I travelled all over Australia to visit them as a client. As I visited each one, I looked at how they worked and I realised that if I was to do this work I needed to define a set of rules for myself.

No drugs (ever in my life), no alcohol, only clean, organic food, no sugar and no processed food. I still maintain these rules 30 years later. I knew that the clearer my body the clearer I would be as a channel for my work and the easier it would be to let go of the negative energy I might encounter through my clients. The commitment to having this life style made me realise I needed to live this way for life, not just when I was working. It also made me commit to learning everything I could about spiritual growth and psychic ability. I realised there were negative and positive energies in the universe. I became totally committed to creating a space for my clients where they could create their own destiny based on positive, predictable information that I gave them. Their choices are their own to make, I am only the transmitter of the possibility of an outcome based on psychic and intuitive intelligence.

I have seen Jeannine Kasper work out daily for 1 to 2 hours just to be fit enough to ride a motor bike in her movie Super Moto. It is not only the practice to train the body that works for her but somehow there is the practice of training the mind, and this practice must come first. Without the belief and commitment of the mind there can be no long-term commitment for anything. Setting goals as an achievement will only get you so far. As you achieve or remove yourself from one goal, to move to the next you are setting yourself up for the game of life, rushing from one thing or goal to the next creating stress and madness, missing the knowledge that is to be learned along the way. The ultimate truth is that the journey is more important than the outcome of the goal, even if the goal is worthwhile. The journey is who you become because of the experiences and learning you find on the way. This allows true commitment for the next part of your life.

My decision to write a book started ten years ago. I often wondered why I had not achieved this goal as I thought I was committed. Over the past ten years I have been on a journey to find myself. This journey is now my book and the words written in it. I never gave up the goal to write, I just needed to commit to making my goal achievable and believing that I would meet the right people to help me. I tried several publishers over the years but nothing happened except I spent time and money with no result, but as I look at the journey I realise that my smaller achievements led me to the outcome I have today. I didn't waste my time or my money, and I learnt a lot about what I did and did not want in my book. I also learnt that my goals and accomplishments are not a measure of who I am. I am not a financial, physical, material outcome because of what I have achieved, I am very humble and wise and full of knowledge because of every experience I have lived. I don't measure myself by my achievements but by who I am. This realisation has freed me from society's judgement and expectation that I would have placed on myself even five years ago.

My ultimate goal in this lifetime is to be able to walk from one dimension to the next. I know this is unachievable as a practical action, but it gives me a life-long quest that started when I was five years old and found the Wishing Chair by Enid Blyton. I have never been able to understand why I cannot walk with unicorns or make chairs fly. I have in my mind the vision of my goal and it keeps me committed to my life path, the belief in magic and all that it embraces, whether the magic comes from a child's laughter or from a sci fi movie or book, it doesn't matter. It's the fact that I believe in the first place and am willing to walk the path of being unique and different that makes it all real and worthwhile. The same can be said of Jeannine Kasper with her commitment to her acting and the ability to be able to empathise with the emotions and life of the person in the role she is playing. This in itself is a gift but to be able to understand it and work with it requires true commitment.

I have stayed in the homes of famous, wealthy people who on the outside look like they have an amazing life full of glamorous events and beautiful clothes. What everyday people don't see is the hours of hard work and commitment that is the product behind the success and the lifestyle. I have seen actresses work out with their trainers for up to 3 hours every day for months just to be fit and strong and to have a specific body shape for a movie role. They have a diet that they adhere to, change their speech, hair or whatever it takes. They also have a business to run, which is them, and involves a lot of appointments and people. If they didn't commit they would not create their dreams.

The amount of success you have in life depends on you. I'm not talking about society's version of success: the big house, the big credit card debt, the lifestyle that is a lie. I'm talking about the success of feeling great about yourself and what you do, which in turn creates a place where you can have the home, family lifestyle you dream about without the stress because you are suppressed and unhappy in some aspect of life. The best thing you can do for yourself and everyone else is GIVE UP the chasing of success based on society's version of it. It's not a real word, you cannot hold it in your hand, it's not tangible, it's false. You will chase it your whole life and never catch it because there will always be someone else's version of success that you see or are compared with and you will feel like a failure then push yourself even harder to chase a different success. Take time to write your goals that you have or have not achieved and then look at the journey you have been travelling and give yourself a positive pat on the back as you embrace the knowledge and wisdom of who you have become as a person. I guess what I'm trying to say is that your soul needs a purpose, it needs a reason to grow and shine. Your physical material self can create all sorts of amazing results, money, cars, houses or whatever you want, but without a greater commitment to a life of meaning and fulfilment there is no true happiness or joy. The commitment to the soul path journey can be different and varied, it may be something as simple as saving the dolphins or the trees, but it must be something bigger than yourself and your needs. This commitment will give you the journey and the journey will give you the experiences to become wise and understanding of your life and its purpose.

Don't let the small negative picture stop you from trusting the magnificent portrait the universe has already painted for you that is just around the corner.

YOUR SOUL PATH YEAR

I created soul path years based on soul path numbers. I created these numbers to help me understand the cycles of life and how they work. People ask if it is numerology; no, it is not. I needed something to help me understand how the universe works it sequence and the parallel connection to my clients lives.

Some years are better than others to create change and stay committed. The following may help you to figure out when to make changes and transformations. Remember, this is only a guide. I always look at every aspect when I am working out my next project.

To work out your soul path year, add your birthday day and month with the year you are in.

Example

Your birthday is 12/05 and the year is 2017, then it is 12+5+2017 which =1+2+5+2+0+1+7=18 which equals 1+8=9 so your soul path year is 9.

Your birthday is 1/1 and the year is 2019 then it is 1+1+2+0+1+9=14 then add together 14= 1+4 =5 your soul path year is 5.

Sometimes if your birthday is near the middle of the year the previous soul path year may overflow into the next, giving you a little of both. This can be positive as it allows a little more time to devote to positive life path choices. If you are procrastinating and are behind the time-line of where you should be, work out where you are up to and step up the game to the next level by looking at the guide for your year. I have had some people up to two years behind and as soon as I point it out to them they know the exact day they did not make the decision or choice to move forward. They then have a choice about catching up or staying stuck in limbo.

SOUL PATH YEARS

SOUL PATH YEAR 1

The beginning of a new cycle. This year is the time to step up and reinvent yourself and transgress to the next level of your soul self. You may have time alone this year but not necessarily be by yourself. This is the year after the transformation or change, after the tsunami. You will need to let go of the old ways this year if you want your life to be different. A perfect year to reinvent yourself. New self-image, career, more responsibility. This is the year you must make the decision to stop climbing the stairs and get in the lift, remembering that if you do, you will leave a lot of people behind because they choose to climb the stairs and do it the hard way. You can separate yourself from the changes that happened last year and move on. The changes last year will allow you to start a new life for yourself based on your needs for the first time in your life. In the past, you have lived according to the rules of society, partners, siblings, parents and many others. This is the time to reinvent yourself based on who you are for yourself from the heart without the outside influence and restraints of past control. You have lived from the outside in, now it is time to live from the inside out by following your heart and trusting in yourself instead of in others.

SOUL PATH YEAR 2

A two soul path year is very busy - I call it the year of the Ferris wheel. You are the wheel and the people around you are in the capsules. As the wheel stops some will get off and some new people may get on. Some will leave of their own accord and others you will remove or leave behind as they are no longer relevant to your life. A year of progress and rapid change. Travel overseas usually happens in a two year or a big house or career move. These adventures also change the people around you. As the people get on and off the wheel it spins faster, making it a busy time. A good year to make sure you are grounded. Year two is the year of the family, a great time to have babies or sort out family issues and have family gatherings.

SOUL PATH YEAR 3

This is the year of the Roller Coaster, up and down. For most of you it will be a good time to rest after last year and reassess the changes that have taken place. Take time to study or research your choices for the future. Money is usually good in a three year but like everything else, it can be up and down. Use this year to be aware of your gifts and talents and how they relate to your passion. It's important to stay focused on the future and keep balanced emotionally. By using the down time to heal, make positive choices, rest and release stuck emotions or life patterns, you will create a smoother path. Try not to let your emotions and thoughts bring you down, stay focused and look to physical exercise to keep you grounded and focused. Don't take on the problems of those around you who are needy; the burden will cause you to lose yourself and it will be difficult to rebuild momentum. This is a perfect year to study, enrol for courses, find your personal branding, decide your own recipe for life and sell it to the world.

SOUL PATH YEAR 4

This is the year of the house of mirrors, everywhere you look you will see your own reflection. As this happens you will need to make decisions and choices about yourself. The difference between these decisions is that you will not be able to change your mind once you have decided and committed. If you decide to sell your home or end a relationship you will not be able to go back. This is a year to fix any health problems you have, even minor ones. If you stepped up the physical exercise last year it will be easier to commit to taking care of your physical body this year. A great year to quit smoking or give up bad habits. The four year is hard work, only because you will need to be fully committed to the choices you made last year. Not a great year to have babies as it could be a little hard on the physical body. A perfect time to build a foundation for your future. Decisions this year should be about lifestyle. Choose where you want to live, how you want to live and what lifestyle makes you happy. Choosing the life that makes you happy will open the doors for future happiness. If your heart lives by the ocean and you are in the middle of a large city, your heart will not sing. Make the choice this year to change your lifestyle and start the wheels in motion. It may take three or four years to manifest but if you stay focused it will happen. The commitments of this year open the door to amazing possibilities and adventures in your 5 year.

SOUL PATH YEAR 5

This is possibly my favourite year. It's full of opportunities and lots of new adventures and choices. A year of rewards for all the hard work and commitment from last year. This is a time for you to stand on top of the stairs and look ahead at the many paths open to you, plenty of invitations and offers around your work and personal life. Enjoy the new lifestyle you have chosen and make future choices based on your happiness rather than because of the need to please others. Accept as many social invitations as you can and enjoy the ride. Be aware of your needs as you choose which path you want to travel, remember if you are happy everyone around you will be happy. Use your intuition to help you decide which career offer or relationship is perfect for you. This is a year when some people decide to leave the earth if they have had a long illness and cannot cope with the world any longer. It's also a time when you can choose to change your lifestyle choices from negative to positive, productive choices.

SOUL PATH YEAR 6

It's important to find your voice and create clarity through loving communication this year. For a long while you have been working, studying, healing or finding yourself. This is a perfect time to bring everything together and present it to the world. If you want to be famous or noticed, this is the time to take advantage of the opportunities that were presented last year and put them to work for you. A perfect year to bring your gifts and talents together. Decide which ones represent you the best and the ones you are good at and sell them to the world. If you are clear about who you are and how you can use your gifts and talents, you can ask for a promotion or more money. A great time to learn to say no to the people in your life who waste your time. You cannot change anyone so don't even try. Say no and spend the time doing something special for yourself. This is the perfect year to shine and to make yourself the most important person in your own life.

SOUL PATH YEAR 7

This is a big year, emotional, sensitive life reflections, spiritual growth, spiritual information downloads, heightened intuition, what am I here for, who am I, what is this life all about, what am I doing…these are all thoughts and concepts for a seven year. The most successful way to stop yourself from travelling down the path of self-analysis is to be very focused on your physical and material world. Be very aware of your finances and your physical health. This will keep you grounded. The emotional downloads are going to happen anyway so you may as well be strong and grounded so you can make sound decisions based on logic and not fear and emotions. If you are looking to change your work, place your intention on the position or choice that provides you the most financial reward. It will lead you to the right people to create your dreams and build strong foundations for your future. This is a year to trust the process, don't listen to the nagging negative voice within, go for the money. Know that this year all your Angels have lined up to help and support you. Staying focused on finances and making money will stop the emotional roller coaster where you can lose focus and motivation. A lot of life issues may evolve around you. It's important to keep your distance and let everyone take responsibility for themselves. This is a year some people choose to leave earth and join the Angels.

SOUL PATH YEAR 8

Soul path year 8 is very powerful. If you stayed on the path last year and didn't succumb to the emotional bullets this will be a very successful year. A time where money will just manifest, you will need to stay focused and balanced so you don't have a physical burnout because it will be busy. Stay on top of your health and fitness, if you started last year you will be fine. I call this the year of the magician, anything can happen, a lot of people meet and commit to a life partner in their 8 year. You can make or lose your money so be aware of what is going on in your finance department and keep everything in perspective. This is a great time to step up and find your power and presence and commit to who you are. The last 7 years come together this year and you will start to see through clean windows where you are going and how it can be achieved, the support and finances will be there to help. Not such a great year to have a baby as it can be taxing and hard work on the physical body, ok to fall pregnant. A 2,3,5,7 or 9 year are better for babies. An 8 year is the perfect time to fix little things that are bothering you physically. Save money this year to make the transformational changes next year easier.

SOUL PATH YEAR 9

If you have been progressively aware over the past 8 years and have looked through the clean windows last year and made some choices based on your intuition and your heart and not based on society and what you think you need to do, then you will be happy with the results of this cycle of change. This is the year God can pick your life up and shake it around in a box until the things and people that are no longer relevant to your future fall out. If you have clean windows you can tell him where you want the box to go, if not, you will just have to wait for the dust to settle and sift through the mess. Think of your life as a movie that has been written for you by everyone else, your parents, employer, partner, neighbours; the movie has been completed, you are the main actor, you have acted how you were scripted to act, now the movie is finished, everyone has left, this is the time you can choose to sit down and write your own script based on who you are for the first time in your life. If you decide to stay in the mess you may be stuck there for another 9 years, until the next cycle starts. Remember if you decide to step up you will leave a lot of people behind, and will very likely change house, job or postcode, maybe everything. You can choose to close the door on the past and embrace your future in a more positive and powerful way. Tie up any loose ends, complete any projects you can and prepare for the next exciting adventure and reinvention of yourself as you step in to the next cycle. If you are destined to have completion this year and you are in denial, your life may be picked up, put in a shoe box shaken around and dropped anywhere. You will need to let the dust settle and see what happens before making choices. We have all seen this happen to others on occasion, they have had some life changing event that has forced them to change their life.

What are your fears? Write down a list of the worst-case scenarios that can happen if you follow your dream.

Once you write down your fears you will see that they are not real and you are stressing and fearful about something that may never happen.

Scarlett Vesper

"When I first met JeanClare I was quite lost about where I was in my life and it's always great to get some hope that things will be okay! She was more than that, she dug down to find the cause of the issue and worked with me and my spirit to find out what I needed to know about myself in order to move forward. As a psychic, she was accurate and definitive in her advice which I love. Jeannie was also the only person who actually was there for me in a situation where I truly needed help, very rare in this day and age. Her kindness and strength is so inspiring and precious to have when we are on the path to have a life we love.

LOVE DREAM BELIEVE. For many years, this was my motto. I know that the most important part of any personal development is to have self-love, in fact learning to love yourself is the glue to every other useful tool. Yes, these are all tools, tools to being a human being. Dreaming was easy for me, I always had a dream, in fact I was in a dream a lot of my youth, escaping the reality I didn't like when I was young. I am also a very visual person, so I can see everything in my mind, even when I work, it's a vision and it's rich and it's clear. Belief, now here is the showstopper, how do you believe in something when in your heart, you don't? When I was little, and I start there because that's where it all begins, our beliefs, our concepts about who we 'think' we are. So when I was little, I believed in magic, my dreams kept me in joy and love and inspired me to be something beyond the human chaos of emotionality. I believed in something greater than myself and I had some part to play, I just didn't know what it was. However, as I started school and meeting other children, I learnt things about me just from their reactions. And so it began...I didn't believe I was lovable, I didn't believe I was worthy, I didn't believe I had what people wanted. I didn't believe in me.

I've done a lot of personal development and all my teachings and understanding leads me to know that our external world often reflects our internal thinking or belief and so somewhere inside, I had this already programmed into my mind. My mother never had a great deal of confidence, but she was strong and didn't let her emotions stop her achieving what she wanted and my dad was the most intelligent man I ever knew, but had no self-belief – a lot of ego, but not a true self confidence to sit in a space of allowance and compassion. Someone of true confidence doesn't have to defend, justify or prove anything to anyone – I work towards that every day. Yes, we are born with our beliefs, they shape our lives and they shape our choices. For many years I believed I was not worth a lot, but somewhere inside, I loved who I was, it was like a secret I couldn't tell anyone and I had to hide that strength, power and self love because I would be seen selfish or self-centred. So this love became personal, it because my best friend and my internal voice of trust and inspiration. I also had the love of many dear friends who fed my self-belief, building a strong foundation and all the while I continually asked the question why was I here and what was my purpose? How could I be happy? How could I be the best I could be? It's been a long standing yearning to this very day.

When you allow things to flow, no resistance, just an open heart and the ability to be discerning and intuitive about the choices you make, then it will 'feel' good and right and it will flow. For me, giving up is saying 'I've given up on living.' I'll never give up because I love life with all its challenges, pain and love and there is no other choice for me. My dark days have been VERY dark and I've felt very alone and afraid. At one point when we had lost everything, I was in the shower thinking, they can take everything, but they can't take ME, my soul, my talent, my heart, my essence. From that day on, my life turned around, financially yes, but I had a big shift about honouring myself and truly understanding that self-belief and self love comes from something much bigger than money or position. A wisdom grows from knowing your true nature and that teaching permeates in everything you do from that moment. My experiences are part of who I am, the challenges are part of my teachings for others and I infuse compassion and love into all that I do."

Scarlett Vesper

I loved working with Scarlett. She was an inspiration and allowed me to push myself to the next level of my journey.

Chapter 5

INTEGRITY

Elyse Taylor

Chapter 5

INTEGRITY

Elyse Taylor

(Australian supermodel living in New York)

Elyse Taylor is one of Australia's most successful exports. She has been a Victoria Secret Angel and the face of Estee Lauder and Nude by Nature to name just a few of her successful campaigns.

I have only been connected to Elyse in the past couple of years. From our first conversation I knew she was a person of integrity. Being true to herself and believing in self-empowerment has been her journey for some time now. The need to be true to her destiny and to herself creates a space in her life for her to have unconditional love for her daughter and an amazing friendship with her mother. Her radiant beauty is her tool for success and is something that she accepts and appreciates, not only with her work but also on a personal level. How she represents herself on a professional level is how she presents herself at all times. The ability to live in two worlds can be difficult; the world of career and the world of being a human. With the ability to know herself Elyse moves from one world to another without the pretence of being false or deceptive to herself or anyone else. Her faith in her own intuition gives her power to believe in herself and helps her make decisions about her life that are perfect for her.

I believe integrity is about being true to yourself. It's knowing within your spirit when you are telling or living a lie and pretending you are living in truth. Living in your own integrity can be a difficult way of being, as you grow spiritually, there is an awareness of how you feel. It's this awareness that can be difficult to empower. Sometimes it's easier to live in the existing space than to stay in the awareness. If you wake up in the morning feeling a little down or emotional, it is easier to tell yourself to ignore the feeling and just get on with the day than to look at what is going on in your life and face a truth. Most people don't or won't take the time to consider why they feel how they do. They live in society's lie that you keep going, don't rock the boat, or question life. Just being aware of WHY you feel or act, how you do can sometime release the baggage. It's like the bump on the road, the first time you drive over it can be upsetting, but the awareness of the bump can allow you to look at ways of driving over it a better way in the future. The answer is not to avoid or ignore it because the consequences will just keep reoccurring.

It's all about hiding truth and keeping secrets which eventually bring your world tumbling down. If you are portraying yourself as a spiritual and truthful person with a hidden agenda there is a lack of integrity lifestyle. There needs to be a truth in who you are as an authentic person. It's the same with money. There cannot be a pretence of saving the world if it's all about making money. Being in your truth is how you save your soul and body from self-destruction. Every time you go against your intuition and knowing, you give away a little piece of who you are and your power to be true to yourself. Integrity grows with self-acceptance. To be someone special do something you don't know how to do, start living outside of the walls and the life you created for yourself. You don't have to be famous or wealthy to live in your own integrity. Taking one step at a time and believing in your intuition is the answer.

It's very easy to sabotage your own integrity by being a people pleaser or by putting other things before yourself. I believe saying no and being true to what you know is self-empowering, not selfish. It is a pleasure to work with Elyse and share my thoughts with her. She takes the relevant information and moves forward by making her own choices that are true to who she is. There is no pretence or procrastination, just being true to the journey and her own reality.

Your contract with the God, Gods of your choice.

THE AKASHIC RECORDS

It has been believed for hundreds of years that there is a supreme force or being that holds records of the patterns, thoughts and future of the Universe, recording each birth, death and their destiny. The records are a compendium of all thought processes and experiences and exists on the astral plane. Imagine it to be a giant record hall filled with rolls of movie film that somehow overlap each other and are interconnecting on every level. I believe there is a network system that brings people together and connects psychic links that are like radio waves that transmit psychic frequencies of thought and desire. I cannot decide if these links are predestined or not but everything I have experienced in my life shows clearly that there are no accidents, everything is exactly as it should be at any given time on our destiny path.

I remember about two years after I had my car accident I visited a numerologist friend of mine for a session. I hadn't seen her for quite some time and was excited to catch up with her personally and to also have a session. The first startling piece of information she gave me was that I had a near death experience on the exact day of my accident. I was gobsmacked. I knew she was good at what she did, and I also knew that she did not know about my accident, so this was a shock. It made me look at all aspects of my life and realise that everything is a pattern and the information we seek is out there. The important insight in all of this for me was that I had a choice about the quality of life I could live. I could still complete my work with spirit helping people and I believe that is the reason I am on this earth, but it also allowed me to realise that I could make a bigger difference if I allowed my negative beliefs about myself to disappear.

Working with Orlando and Miranda was the beginning of this for me. They saw my gifts and talents as special, recognising them as a reflection because they recognise and accept their own unique and special gifts and qualities. People ask me how I met Miranda Kerr. The answer is, I allowed myself to follow my intuition. I had been working as a clairvoyant for about twenty years and had decided to have a break. I left the healing centre I was working at and worked in a dress shop travelling around Australia working at some of their different stores. I loved the position because it allowed me to talk to women on a different level and I have always loved the fashion industry. One day I was walking past the same centre I had left previously and a voice in my head told me it was time to go back and ask for a space to work from. Now this was hard for me because I did not like the staff or the energy of the shop, but I went back and humbly asked for a space. They were very gracious and gave me Saturdays. The second Saturday I was there, I was booked out and didn't take much notice of who had booked to see me. A couple of weeks later I had Miranda book in. One of the staff quietly asked if it was the famous Miranda Kerr. I was unsure myself. As it turned out it was the beautiful Miranda. She had been given my name by her aunt who had seen me on the second Saturday. Miranda returned to New York, she met Denise Vassi at a yoga class and gave my number to Denise, who gave it to Yael Lilienfeld and Alina Puscau who gave it to Jeannine Kaspar who gave it to Luke Gottwald and they all in turn have given it to dozens of other people they know in N.Y. and L.A.

I was destined to meet Miranda who ultimately nearly seven years later lead me to Elyse Taylor. I also believe you can change your contract, whether it is with yourself or a god it does not matter. Your destiny will be the same, it's just that you have better options. It may mean better finances, health, love, support, peace, harmony, whatever you decide you need to live a better life.

CONTRACT 1

Your Name.

Just because we are given a specific name at birth it doesn't mean we can't change the contract, let's face it, a birth certificate is a contract.

I believe that if you don't like your name you need to change it. If you like your name and your life is just not working out how you need it to, then change the spelling of your name to create a different frequency. Some of you may just decide to change your name or how it is spelt because of the numerology factor. I did this about two years ago and my life has changed dramatically. I choose to take on my mother's surname and let go of my father's surname. My father's name held a lot of sad memories and from a numerological point of view was a very difficult path. I made a choice to let the name go. That decision changed everything. I decided to take my mother's maiden name which is powerful, it gives me great memories and I love the sound of it and how it reminds me of my grandmother. It also has a much better result with the numerology pattern. I have noticed in the time since then that not reading, hearing and signing my old name has released me from the triggers connected to the memories entwined with that name. Before I went through the changing process I meditated on it, had myself balanced through kinesiology to accept the new name on all levels and checked with the numerologist. It's not an accident that some famous people change their name and find fame. There are lots of great books out there on this subject. The Romance In Your Name by Juno Jordan and The Life You Were Born To Live by Dan Millman are two that I love.

CONTRACT 2

Contract number two is a different game altogether. I believe we come here with an agreement or contract with the universe to do specific things. I believe that the universe sits on a brick wall and every child that comes into the world is like a brick, they are shaped and have a purpose that keeps everything working and balanced and keeps the wall from falling down. I have also noticed over the years of speaking with Angels and spirits who have passed over that we seem to have a destined birth and death date. I know that sometimes there can be an accident but in general its predestined.

This is your destiny contract where you need to literally sit down and write a letter to God and tell him what you need. This is serious business because what you write is what you will get. I remember I did this with a client in Los Angeles to change business strategies because a lot of the people he found were not authentic and had low levels of truth and integrity. We rewrote his contract and created a paragraph about him creating authentic, honest and real business deals and partners. Over the next eighteen months a lot of deals fell through before they got off the ground, he rang me to ask what was going on, I reminded him of his contract and when we looked at the deals that fell over it became clear that the people concerned were not authentic and honest to the level he needed them to be and were looking to make money however they could.

To better understand how the Akashic records work I suggest you watch the movie The Adjustment Bureau with Matt Damon. It will sort of show you how your destiny is supposed to be set out and the files and maps are held in the Akashic library. I believe to live in integrity you need to feel that your life is RIGHT for you. If you don't fit or feel you don't belong you will try to change things that are not meant to be changed or do things that will sabotage who you can be and what you can create for yourself. The big thing about the records is that there is a register of every good and bad thing that you have done to yourself and anyone else. This record is kept forever and comes back to you as KARMA. I don't necessarily believe that we create bad Karma and need to repay others back for bad deeds, I believe it is more about the lessons we need to learn from what we have or haven't created at some time in our life/lives. I also believe that every deed we have created that is self-indulgent and harmful to others disempowers us and creates fractures in our soul/spirit. Every time we go against our intuition we give our power away and create a break within ourselves. I have spoken to many people who have gone through with a certain decision knowing in their heart that it is wrong but they do it anyway. So many people have walked down the aisle to marry someone and in their heart, knew it was not the best choice for them, it always ends in disaster, and it always stays with them as a bad intuitive feeling that they knew about and didn't trust. Being true to yourself is paramount and believing in yourself is paramount, it takes a lot of courage to have integrity with your word to yourself and others. How many times have you said to yourself or to someone else I won't do that again only to repeat the pattern?

Who you are as an adult can be your own choice. As a child, you are shaped and moulded by the people around you. Growing into adulthood you chose what you could and could not accept responsibility from that learning. The older you are the more the obligation is yours to accept total responsibility for your own choices and actions. Be very clear in your letter to God about what you need. After my car accident I decided to give up my clairvoyant work because I didn't want the same lifestyle I had experienced in the past. I meditated and prayed for answers and the words came to me very clearly that I could inspire people to believe in themselves by giving them a glimpse of the future and letting them know that they have a destiny but they also have choices. They have their own power, they just need to believe. I knew I did not want to just give predictions about who someone will marry or that they will win the lottery, to me that was a waste of time, I needed to give them more. I rewrote my contract and requested a different type of client. I stated that I would only work with clients who wanted to transform their lives and create a world that would help others. I also stated that I would not continue if I had to struggle financially. I needed to grow and evolve with every client, for every appointment to mean something. To this day, I often write letters to God for other people and put them in my bible. The prayer is always answered, sometimes I forget and find the letters months later only to realise that the request was granted. To do more work with your contract check my website for information on the release of my work book: www.jeanclare.com.au.

THE PERCEPTION OF THE MIRROR

Your mind tells you stories every day. The mirror is a classic example of this deception. Some mirrors create the illusion of being slim, some are an almost true reflection. When you look in the mirror your thoughts tell you how you look. What you need to remember is that when you look in the mirror and think your image is great and then go into an environment where you may not feel comfortable, your thoughts will forget the positive image you saw in the mirror and you will start to doubt yourself because of how you feel and the past memories you have recorded in your mind. You may even look at other people's appearances and compare yourself. There are other times when you feel wonderful, look in the mirror and realise you have coffee on your nose and it's been there for ages. Your thoughts reflect how you feel and what you tell yourself about who you are. Sometimes your reflection and thoughts are a result of your environment. If you had a hundred mirrors and you placed them in different places around the world and could see your image in each mirror, the background of each reflection would give you a completely different image each time for each mirror. This is true with life; if you are living in a negative environment you will be moulded by that environment and reflect those negative feelings in the mirror as an image of who you are. If you grew up with a consciousness of poverty it will be reflected in your thoughts about yourself every day. If you grew up in an environment of violence that will affect how you feel and behave. Children who grow up with drug addict parents always reflect that frequency even if they are against drug use. They will always know that the parents love and need for drugs was a higher priority than the love for the child they are supposed to nurture and protect.

The healing of the self-image is about seeing the person within, not the person outside of who we think we are. The words of criticism from parents or someone else usually depict the outside image. This image is recreated by negative memory recall. A person who experiences inner peace and self-acceptance has one image when they look at who they are. The outer reflection is a representation of the inner glow and happiness and the inner image is embraced as a collection of the positive aspects of that person's soul, creating a mirror ball effect.

CREATE CONVERSATIONS THAT MATTER

Sometimes the best and most effective conversation is silence.

I have learned with my grandchildren the most effective communication is silence; the power to listen is far greater than the power to make a comment. The ability to listen and reply, what a wonderful idea or you are clever, lifts their spirit and allows them to feel powerful. They need to chat about everything and anything, sometimes to the extent that I suggest we watch television or listen to music just to escape. They have amazing imaginations and nothing interferes with their ability to create words that have no meaning to us as adults but fills their world with possibility and magic. We know there are three main senses, seeing, hearing and feeling. Most humans have two primary senses. Hearing, feeling or seeing, feeling the people who are hearing, seeing are usually extremely intelligent and don't have much awareness of emotions and how they affect us. It's a handy thing to know about people you are dealing with because it's no use talking to someone for an hour, giving instructions. If they are visual they won't have heard a word you have said. Seeing or visual people usually have vivid imaginations, they can picture things in their mind as soon as they think about them. Give them a plan and they can see the outcome straight away. There is no guarantee that their vision will be the same as yours, but it will be very close. Have you ever wondered why your children who play a lot of computer games never hear you talking to them and need to have the volume very loud? It's because they are usually seeing, feeling. They can feel the next move in the game and see the plan or pattern of the players. Designers, hairdressers, nail technicians, surgeons, anyone who works with their hands and eyes are usually seeing, feeling. Ever wondered why your hairdresser never listens to you when you tell her how you would like your hair? She already has a picture of what she will do as soon as you sit down.

Audio people don't usually have the ability to see the big picture on paper - they like to hear the plan and think about it, they may take notes so they have a better picture of what's going on. Counsellors, psychologists, nurses, good retail staff anyone who needs to hear what you say is usually audio; they are good at listening. A general medical practitioner is a classic example. They will listen to what you say, ask for the symptoms, then think about it, write some notes then tell you what is wrong with you. A visual doctor asks to see the problem, touches it then asks about the symptoms. He will then get on his computer, maybe look at your medical history and make a diagnosis. When you are having communication with someone, start to become aware of their actions. If their listening span is only a couple of minutes, they are probably visual so you know you are wasting your time on words.

AUTHENTIC COMMUNICATION

Authentic communication is about your reaction to the other person's words and the creation of a space to hear their words without judgement. In other words, their communication will usually be about themselves not you. I am forever saying to clients who recite negative communication about what someone else has said, what is the real meaning of what they are trying to say, what do they need?

Over the past 30 odd years I have seen a lot of different people from different walks of life all over the world. 95% of you come to me about your life, confused, unhappy, not sure of direction, why are you not achieving your desired results and mixed up in all of that is the complaint about someone else. This person is doing this or that and that means I can't have my success. There is only a minor group of you who have not complained about the OTHER person. They are the ones who succeed. They come to me and say I'm not sure about or how do I transform this aspect of my life? Strangely, they are usually young men. Now I love how we have a complaining button that we press and use to justify why we can't get what we want.

ONCE YOU HAVE YOUR LIFE IN ORDER AND TAKE RESPONSIBILITY FOR YOUR LIFE CHOICES YOU START TO LIVE IN THE VIBRATION OF YOUR TRUE SELF.

With INTEGRITY comes responsibility. You are responsible for every thought in your head, every word you speak, every action you take on every level, ultimately you are responsible for you and your life and how you live it. You can blame everyone else as much as you like but deep inside you know it is a lie and as long as you live in that lie you are not living with truth or integrity. It's your choice to decide about who you want and need to be to create the life you would love. If you dislike your work situation and complain about it a lot, look at why you stay there. Write down the reasons you don't leave, be truthful about it with yourself. Look at courses you can do to change things, or establish yourself financially to be ready for change.

The conscious and subconscious lies your brain will tell you about yourself and your life.

FINANCIAL FREEDOM

Financial Freedom. Society and your brain will tell you that financial freedom is not attainable. You have been brainwashed to believe you must spend money you don't have and it's ok because everyone else does it. Your money is your energy. You have expanded energy to make the money and it is an extension of you. The bank accounts are in your name, the taxation files are in your name, so you are responsible for your own financial situation. You even choose the bank, and the wallet to hold your money and cards. One of the most courageous things you can do in this lifetime is CUT up your credit cards.

I remember years ago, I was looking to lose weight and someone told me to write down everything I put in my mouth for 30 days. I did this and was astounded when I looked at the list after a week. Do this with your money. Write down every single transaction you make for a month including automatic payments from your bank account, also costs for your phone, electricity and other utilities, junk food, everything even if its two dollars for a bottle of water or a pack of gum. If you complain about your boss or wages look at how you are acting in the issue. If it's not transformable, leave. Your work is the one thing that rules your emotions in every aspect of your life.

Emotional pain is the hardest of all. To those who have experienced the feeling of deep loss there are no words on earth that can ever express how you feel. The tears, feeling empty and fearful, are like a deep bottomless pit. Once you start to spiral downwards it's hard to find your wings and fly back to your plane of existence in the real world. Filling your life with material goods will not help. You would be better off using the money to pay for healing and learning. The power of financial freedom is something that not many humans experience. I often wonder if some of you create financial stress so you have a reason to live, work and exist because maybe there is nothing else worthy in your life and it gives you a reason to get out of bed. To have a perfect home, car, career is the ultimate and perfect dream so long as you don't mortgage your soul and spirit to the bank to pay for a lifestyle. There comes a time in life when you need to ask yourself what your time is worth and how you can create freedom of life and living. Why waste time and energy on something you don't want? What is your freedom and self-expression worth to you and how do you put a value on yourself? You can control your money or you can allow your money to control you.

CRYING

When you are small you are told not to cry, it's ok, everything will get better so you withhold the tears until the dam overflows and the tears are uncontrollable. This usually happens after a crisis. You feel as though there is something wrong with you because you cry all the time and feel miserable. Then your brain steps in and tells you to get better or to give up.

A good cry releases some of the mental hurt. Your brain will make the tears and say, "Ok you are sad, upset and crying, so that should fix things so you can get on with life." I will let you have more sessions of crying but only every now and then. I will allow you to feel guilt, sadness and misery but only on my terms and by my thoughts. If you really want to give up I will create a whole month, year or forever for you to use as justification for not living life and being happy, after all how can you feel happy when you are in such misery and everything is going wrong?

ANGER

The anger comes sometimes before or after the crying. It is the brain allowing you to blame someone else because life didn't go how you assumed it would and your vision of the future didn't go according to plan. You can't be upset forever because something or someone left you or let you down, but you can create hate and jealousy as the primary emotion to justify why you feel like you do. Let's vent our anger on the person who loves us the most, because they are most likely to forgive us for our actions.

SURRENDER

This comes after the anger. You bury the loss and anger deep inside and move on with life carrying a broken heart and soul because your brain says, you can't deal with the release of the pain because you don't know how, so you need to put it in a box and hide it. Let's just pretend we are ok and the pain and the memory will go away. If we work hard and keep busy we won't have time to stop and feel our pain and loss. Reading this paragraph may mean it's time for you to surrender, let go of the need to control your emotions and your life. Remember life passes with time and surrendering yourself to yourself is the ultimate step on the journey of self-acceptance. Accepting that you may be in love with the idea of a perfect and controlled life is very powerful. The idea is not real and controlling every emotion is not real; it's your idea of survival, a picture in your head of how your life should look. Have a look at nature and start spending time with trees, grass, stars, flowers, waterfalls and anything pertaining to nature on a regular basis and it will help you surrender. There is no control over the weather, waves, rain or wind. By connecting to the elements you will feel more connected to the world you live in.

FREEDOM

We are amazing creatures, we can create all sorts of reasons to live in a toxic environment. The thought of being free and happy is our ultimate dream, but we block the possibility of freedom, with thoughts of responsibility and the non-existent terrible consequences of a future outcome caused by rash behaviour if we leave a secure situation to follow our dream. Staying in a work situation or a toxic relationship are classic examples. People who stay in a work situation just to pay the bills usually have an unhealthy young or old age. Giving up on the dream creates emotional pain.

The pain eats away at you your whole life and you finally:

1. You become sick. Depression, cancer, exhaustion, diabetes, etc.

2. Leave your partner/family.

3. Make very bad life choices/drugs, alcohol, medication.

4. Sabotage your career/life.

The clients who come to me the unhappiest are the ones who never followed their career dream, or married their first love. They know the exact moment they turned their back on their dream to make someone else happy or to not cause an upset.

By being truthful to yourself and living in your own integrity you must believe and trust in the knowing of who you are and believe there is a much greater force that designs your destiny. Every time I doubt the universe or whoever, I don't know who or what is out there, but there is a divine force that cannot be ignored. Step up to your truth and own your life; don't let past pain stop you.

When someone leaves your life, or something you have worked for and believed in doesn't succeed and you feel lost and empty, how do you go on? Where do you find the tools to keep believing and never give up? There is a reality at times that you may have been in love with the vision you have of a person and not in love with the real person at all. This will often lead to heartache because the vision is constantly shattered and you keep rebuilding it to suit yourself, which is not the true picture. As you shatter and rebuild, you lose part of yourself with every illusion. There comes a time when you must let go of the idea and look at reality. Allowing others to be free to express themselves gives you the power to be free as well. The need to change or control everything and everyone in your life will ultimately lead to something breaking, probably you. Your thoughts are what control your actions, your actions control your ability to create freedom. Freedom of self-expression gives you the power to not worry about what others think about you and what you do. Mel Gibson's version of Hacksaw Ridge is a classic example. Desmond Doss was a simple man, pure of heart who believed in his own word to his God, which allowed him to have freedom of thought which ruled his actions, without changing who he was because of the judgement of other's (great movie).

It helps to remember that every day the sun will shine, the flowers will bloom, the sky will be blue, the waves on the ocean will move, babies will be born, seasons come and go and you can't change this, it just happens. As time moves forward you will heal a little bit at a time until one day you feel as though you can let go and be happy and the colours seem brighter, the music louder and you feel closer to your spirit than you have in the past because you have stepped up the ladder of spiritual awareness on the journey of self-discovery.

GUILT

Guilt is the classic emotion that we learn at the youngest age. We are made to feel guilty for being happy, sad, smart, naughty, intuitive and I'm sure there are lots more little things we can feel guilty for. One of the biggest guilts society has created is that we need to feel sad and bad when we don't live up to the expectations of others. Remember guilt is not real, it's a word we made up to use for the expression of a feeling. If the word didn't exist, would you still feel or experience it in the real world? No matter how well they get on and how much love is involved, most children feel a little guilty because they think their parents are strange creatures who have no idea who their own children are. They think their parents have different belief systems and often veer to the weird side of things with no idea of what they are talking about. Given a choice they would rather spend time with their friends than their parents. Parents look at their children and wonder what planet they came from, why their ears and eyes don't work. They try very hard to show the child how the brain is supposed to work and how they should live their life, forgetting that the child already knows and usually figures it out before the parent even knows what is happening.

I look at the concept of the journey we take on every day and realise that life is a game and it is meant to be enjoyed. The creation of society and the falseness of being perfect is overriding the enjoyment and gratitude of just breathing and having two feet on the ground. We are in a constant search for Nirvana and perfection, both of which we already have. I do not believe we are here to learn LESSONS, in my opinion it's more about acceptance of who we are and understanding ourselves and our place in the universe, the role we play in the survival of the world and mankind. Knowing that in any given instant everything is exactly how it is meant to be, and just because that is how it is today does not mean that's how it will be tomorrow. Belief in the concept of stepping back and knowing there is nothing wrong with you except that you give yourself a hard time and expect everything and everyone to fit into your preconceived mould of how the world should work is your obsession and causes the stress.

All children want from their parents is to be told they are perfect and special, whether it's true or not. If the child believes in themselves that will be their world. All parents want is to see their children happy and to know that as a parent they are not a failure. Whenever the parent looks at the adult child and sees or knows they have money or other issues they feel they have failed the child in some way. Instead they need to let go of feeling responsible and to realise the child is an adult and is now responsible for themselves. Except in certain circumstances, we are not responsible for anyone over the age of 18 or 21, depending on the culture. Once the child reaches that age they are responsible for themselves, every time you criticise, offer advice not asked for, or try to control, you are disempowering them, allowing the space for self-doubt and confusion to manifest. In a similar way the adult/child can punish the parent by needing help and making the parent feel responsible. The child/adult makes the parent prove how much they love them by needing something. Step back at some stage and look at what you feel guilty about, be realistic, look at the concept of it as not being real and let it go. I love writing things down to get them out of my head. If you do this, don't read what you have written, once it's out of your head let it go.

Chapter 6

RESPECT

Orlando Bloom

Chapter 6

RESPECT

Orlando Bloom

Who better to inspire me to write about respect than Orlando Bloom?

People who live in respect don't judge, criticise or put down other people. They have often had an adverse or devastating experience in their life, which makes them appreciate everything they have and who they are. It also helps them to understand the suffering of others.

To have respect for others you must have respect for yourself. We come to realise that if we are to make a difference in the world we must be alive and healthy to do it. I'm sure Mother Teresa realised at an early age that if she was going to help anyone she needed to be alive to do it. Let's face it, you can't save the world if you can't save yourself, or if you are dead.

Respecting the body, mind and spirit takes time and effort. Lots of people out there do spiritual work on amazing levels but they abuse their own body by over indulging in all sorts of things.

Sometimes life is just like a beautiful spider web. We walk along the path and have a feeling there is something up ahead, sometimes we ignore the feeling and keep walking, we walk straight into a sticky spider web. We think, I knew that was there, why did I not listen to my intuition? Then we start to pick off the sticky, messy web, sometimes it's easy, mostly it's not. It's all over us and feels terrible. Other times we see it, look at it and think how amazing and beautiful it is, but then we are not content to stand back and just admire so we poke it and it trembles. Fascinated by the challenge, we go against our knowing and poke it again and a strand breaks and it trembles. Again, not satisfied, we ignore our intuition and poke it again. This time our finger becomes entangled within the web we have woven and we are bitten by the spider. Feeling hurt and defeated, we step back and wonder how could this happen to me? To understand the process of life we need to have respect for the spider (life).

Your body is your temple and your home is your sacred space, your mind is your universe.

ORLANDO BLOOM

I first met Orlando in 2009. The time I spent with him was one of the highlights of my life. He is exactly how he appears to be. He is happy, carefree, down to earth, sensitive and has a powerful personal presence. Orlando respects himself and every living being, not only as a Buddhist practice, but because that's who he is. He is not afraid to be happy, adventurous, successful, searching for answers on how to improve his life in every aspect. If he finds a spiritual modality he doesn't believe in, he doesn't discredit the process, he just notes that it is not for him, but it may suit someone else. He is the same with things in his everyday life. It's called being positive and open to all possibilities and respecting life. He is a very private person, but loves people. One of the most fun times I had in Los Angeles was a stay at Orlando's house in Beverly Hills. He was away at the time and Miranda was having a visit from her mother so she was staying elsewhere in L.A. Orlando's house was beautiful, practical, comfortable and welcoming. Everything reflected love and respect, from his gardens to his furniture. We could tell he loved his home and everything in it.

> " I speak to everyone in the same way, whether he is the garbage man or the president of the university."
>
> ALBERT EINSTEIN

I met Orlando in all different places at different times. No matter where we were or who we were with he was always the same open, happy and good hearted person. The one thing that is paramount with him is his respect for his craft. He does not take his success for granted and works hard to be the best he can be in his career. I believe the accident he had with his back when he was younger gave him the insight he needed to live a life of adventure and fulfilment. It also gave him the ability to respect and cherish everything you are and everything you can be as well as respecting the journey. He could have given up when he had the accident but I don't believe that it was an option he even considered.

Respect allows you to speak to others with patience and understanding without the need to judge or condemn the other person because they don't agree with or understand your request, vision or need. It creates a space for you to be able to listen with a clear vision of the other persons needs without making your own agenda the priority. When you have awareness that the other person is speaking or requesting, you need to know it is their agenda and their situation, not yours. Treating them with respect won't make them feel stupid or insignificant and creates the stepping back for you from their problems that they may be projecting onto you.

Respect is when you truly look at the people you love or care about and ask yourself what do they feel right now and what do they need from me to feel loved and safe. It is not you looking at them and thinking what you need from them or what you need to do or say to get them to do what or to get what you want from them to feel better about yourself. Now would it not be easier to have respect for yourself which would then flow onto other people around you? Is it not easier to look at what you are doing to create the situation in the first place? Take time to look at your day. What you say and how you act toward others is exactly what you will get back from them. Why do you always expect and assume your partner, family, friends should act or behave in a certain way just because that's how you want or believe that's how they should be?

RESPECT MONEY

How many hours a day do you spend stressing about money, your job, and other mundane things that you make more important than your own wellbeing? You waste a lot of time and energy with these thoughts that are not even real. How often do you stop and think about who you love, and how much you love them? If we spent more time thinking about loving and respecting what we have and less time thinking about what we don't have, the world would be a different place. The one thing I realised in the 1980's when I learnt REIKI is that it was ok to feel love for every living thing on earth including myself.

The principles of Reiki are:

1. Just for today DO NOT ANGER.
2. Just for today DO NOT WORRY.
3. Just for today SHOW LOVE AND RESPECT FOR EVERY LIVING THING.
4. Just for today HAVE AN ATTITUDE OF GRATITUDE.
5. Just for today DO YOUR WORK HONESTLY.

DR. MIKAO USUI

We never see anything on commercial television about love and respect, the whole concept of the world today is to have everything instantly, money, success, health, even happy children. There is no guidance out there to teach us how to be patient and work through a process showing respect for whatever you are trying to achieve. We are even told that if we buy a certain motor vehicle we will have happy children. Subconsciously we have the TV commercial in the back of our mind when looking for a new car. That car will not give you a happy family, most of the time it will just cause issues because the children leave a mess in the car and don't understand why it's more important than they are. Respecting yourself takes away the need to sell your life to a bank or a finance company. People do all sorts of weird things just to have money; they steal, sell drugs, kill people and sometimes themselves. They even start wars just for money. Once the need for power or money becomes life consuming, the ability to respect yourself and anyone else disappears. I find it interesting that a lot of very famous and wealthy people are religious. They go to church and pray for guidance. They sit around the dinner table and show gratitude for their meal and for each other. I'm not saying that you need to be religious but I am saying that these people take time to appreciate what God has given them each and every day. When things go wrong and you take time to pray about the issue, something in your mind creates a space for the possibility of an answer in some way, shape or form. It allows the intuition to find a solution in a way that is best for you, not a solution that fixes the issue in an instant without regard for the long term repercussions. Praying is a form of meditating.

Time after time I see young couples working long hours, making great money, living the dream only to lose it all because they are over committed financially. The stress impacts them on every level. The feeling of failure is the hardest of all to deal with. Some men spend their entire life seeking and working to reclaim what they lost. Knowing how much money you have in the bank and how you spend it is not only smart, it shows awareness of the value of money.

To change your money habit you will need to transform your mindset and actions.

Because most of the ideals you have come from your childhood it's easier to follow through with physical actions than try to change a life time of belief patterns.

1. Have a goal to work toward. Something material (holiday, car, house deposit, bed, television).

2. Make it something important.

3. Create a vision board, keep it simple and focus on one item.

4. Start with something small - $10,000 to $50,000.

5. Next to the picture of the item have a space where you can write weekly totals of your savings.

6. Open a bank account away from your regular bank, with no cards attached and if possible, no bank fees.

7. Commit ten percent of your weekly earnings to this account no matter what.

8. Add extra amounts that you may have left over after paying your accounts.

9. Allow yourself to feel good about saving money.

Saving 10% of your gross earnings is like a tithing to yourself, it shows your belief in yourself and the world that you trust the process and know you will be provided for. I was taught by an old Chinese friend about money. She taught me the basics.

To pre-programme your brain, the happy feeling of SAVING must be greater than the need to spend. Always be aware of exactly how much money you have in the bank and how much you owe. Create your own system for paying accounts and list your priorities.

> “Money, Money, Money, manifest thyself right here, right now in rich abundance.”
>
> CATHERINE PONDER

Catherine Ponder's book The Dynamic Laws Of Prosperity is a great read. Her above affirmation works for me every time.

RESPECT YOUR PHYSICAL BODY

The first aspect of respect, I believe, is to know your body. How amazing does it feel to eat the food or do the exercise that you know your body loves and responds to? How great do your clothes fit, your thoughts become positive, levels of happiness grow and your whole life improves?

One thing I noticed when I was staying in Orlando's house is that he had lots of English food in the pantry. I am a true believer that Australians need Aussie food, Chinese need Chinese food, Indians need Indian food and so all the rest of the population. Chinese people generally live a long time in Australia and I think it's amusing that you very rarely see them in a McDonalds or a KFC takeaway place, but you see them in a Chinese restaurant. Know your body and respect it's needs. Remember commercial take away food outlets don't care if they make you unhealthy. They only care about selling you and your children food, the end result for them is PROFIT. They don't even know who you are and they don't care. To them you are a statistic, you are making them wealthy and yourself unhealthy. They don't have a loving connection to their food and that is also a reason it is unhealthy. They don't respect your needs or care about your body; if you don't, why should they? The farmers who grow healthy or organic food love what they do so their products will have a positive response to your body because it's grown with love and care.

Find out your blood type and your genetic ancestry. This will play a major part in how and what you should eat. Your Chinese star sign is also very relevant, if you know your animal and whether you are say a metal or a wood rabbit etc. you will know the basic fundamentals of your own personality. This also relates to the western star signs but I feel they are not as powerful in the personality traits. Another thing we forget about is the season we were born. People born in winter seem to love wholesome warming foods where as those born in the summer months love summer food types. Respecting your physical body creates clarity of thought, good clean food and nutrients nourish the brain and allow it to be healthy. Foggy brain from chemicals, GMO food and other toxic products creates depressive and negative thoughts and behaviour. You will seek a quick fix just to get through the day because you cannot see or think with clarity and lack motivation. It then generates into a repetitive cycle. Feeling foggy equals more junk food, alcohol, drugs and food that your body is sensitive to and it goes on until you make a commitment to love and respect yourself enough to transform how you behave toward yourself.

There is also the aspect of you taking responsibility and not blaming your past or anyone in your life for how you feel. You all know your own bad behaviour pattern. You just need to step up and stop the habit if you desire a healthy successful lifestyle. All the money in the world will not make a difference if you have a sick, tired body. It's scary to think about how many famous, wealthy, successful people have died from drug overdoses in the past 5 years in America. I know destiny is destiny but I often wonder how their lives would have turned out if someone had taught them to respect who they are, to not allow others to disempower them and to not take on opinions that they think other people have of them. A healthy body means a healthy mind. People who starve themselves and don't nourish their body usually finish up exhibiting erratic and crazy behaviour. On the other side there are those of you who work out at gyms to the extreme, spending two or three hours there every day. Everything needs to work in moderation. Make sure you are not spending hours at the gym as a technique to avoid life or other issues at home. Is it worth it to hurt your body just to be a certain way? Everyone is different.

One of the realisations I had at the gym was that I always felt strange after using the machines. One day after I had finished work and I was still in tune I went to a yoga class. I was early so I decided to use the walking machine. As soon as I placed my hands on the bars I felt the energy of the last person who used the machine. This was a shock because I had never thought about it before, but it made sense to me in that instant as to why I had always felt terrible after using equipment at a gym. I looked around the gym and saw frustrated, angry, happy, tired, committed people all using the same equipment and realised that I had been picking up on their energy, and whoever had used the machine I was working out on had left their frequency for me to feel. That awakening helped me in other areas of my life as well, shopping trolleys, petrol pumps, airports, buses, all public places really. I wear gloves as much as I can, wash my hands a lot, especially at airports, and find that wearing a hat in crowds helps turn off the receivers.

RESPECT YOUR HOME

I know lots of people who have a beautiful home and don't respect the space. It doesn't matter if you are renting or it's yours. A home is a reflection of who you are, your life, work, family and how your mind works. I learnt from my Grandmother that you don't need a lot of material goods, you just need the basics that are very good quality and take care of them and they will last you forever. If you buy a lot of cheap products your home will reflect that mass produced energy. High quality products have a different energy and if you take care of them with love and gratitude they will reward you by staying beautiful and productive. It's works to have a balance of high end product and a bit of commercial thrown in just to create variety. Show you love your home by keeping it clean and tidy. The universe has provided you a space to live in; the least you can do is take care of it. You live in a certain home because there is something you need to learn about yourself because of the frequency of the house number.

THE MEANING OF HOUSE NUMBERS

To find the frequency of your house number simply add all the numbers together.

2/56=2+5+6=1+3=4 or 357=3+5+7=1+5=6

If you read about the numbers and decide you need to change the frequency of your home it's an easy thing to do. If you would like to transform the frequency from a 2 house to an 8 house because you need to improve your finances, all you need to do is place the number or letter needed to turn the 2 into an 8. For example you can draw a tiny 6 above or near the 2 on your mailbox or on the house front where the numbers are to change the frequency 2+6=8. Or you can place the corresponding letter next to the 2 in this case an F which has the vibration of 6 to make the house a number 8. This process works very well. I have given it to several people who have been amazed by the outcome.

A=1, B=2, C=3, D=4, E=5, F=6, G=7, H=8, I=9.

NUMBER 1 is a home where you may spend a little time by yourself. Other house members will usually do their own thing. It's a funny number when it comes to being neat and tidy. It can be very calm and tidy or messy and hectic. It doesn't like to be a rental property, and likes to look prestigious. This is a home where everyone forgets to tell each other where they are and what they are doing. It's usually a happy home and loves family. As a rental property it will usually attract single people who rent as a group. A great home for new beginnings.

NUMBER 2 home is always busy, lots of family and friends coming and going, usually ok to keep tidy, but loves attention, a good home for pets. This is also a great home where you can feel safe. Renovations can be tricky in a number 2 because it doesn't like change. Always check water plumbing before buying a number 2. Emotions can run high in this frequency because everyone is busy. Can be a bit of a party house or occupants may play loud music.

NUMBER 3 home is all over the place. It can be a happy space one week then upset and hectic the next. The same goes for being neat and tidy and the flow of money and people. Number 3's like to look lovely on the outside; can sometimes have a messy yard. Potted flowers or brightly coloured outdoor furniture can be the answer to creating a feeling of happiness and ambiance.

NUMBER 4 home can be hard work. It loves committed people who don't change things too much. It is a great house to sort out your career, relationships, money and health. It is usually a very well built and sturdy home. Need to keep the windows clean in this house to create the ability to see clearly. A great home to start a new career or business from. It loves prosperous, hardworking people.

NUMBER 5 is a great house number, there is always something happening, lots of travelling, career changes. New doors opening can be a possibility with this home. Loves people and visitors, is a good investment property so long as the tenants respect the building. This house loves the presence of spirit and allows for lots of dreaming and planning.

NUMBER 6 house can be interesting, quite often low energy and a need to speak up or the opposite can occur, leaving space for upset and arguments. It's a home that should sell or rent easily. Flowers or water features around this home will help keep the energy calm and clear. A number 6 home loves to be noticed because of the beautiful gardens or unique architecture.

NUMBER 7 is usually a calm space and likes peace and quiet. The gardens can tend to be untidy if not loved and nurtured. Not a party home, but does like people. A great house for rest or recuperation, spiritual growth and good neighbours. Loves flowers or trees that encourage nature. This is an easy house to live in if you are a happy person. There is usually an Angel around a 7 home which can create a feeling of peace and harmony. A great house to lay around the pool and relax.

NUMBER 8 is the perfect investment property. It's a strong reliable home, which encourages balance and harmony. Great for making and saving money, or to use as a business base, you will need to be aware of health issues in this house as it has a strong masculine frequency. Loves neat and tidy gardens. It does sometimes needs a lot of attention and does like to have full occupancy. Number 8 doesn't like to be left empty and will quickly fall into disrepair. It loves to look beautiful inside and out. Children love the frequency of this home and can often be noisy and excited. If you are single and live in this vibration then make sure you don't become too isolated. Make sure you do lots of entertaining. This house is the number for making money and creating prosperity.

NUMBER 9 home is a place of endings. It can often be the last rental before people purchase their own home or where relationships end. It usually has a junk room or a few junk draws. A home you need to declutter frequently and can often have lots of children in one room. This is also a house for unexpected visitors. It's usually a happy home and loves candles, incense and flowers. The added number can be small so it doesn't interfere with the mail delivery. I find it easier to add a letter, you can google the value of letters and add the appropriate letter to change the frequency.

A house needs to be a home no matter how many people live in it or how big it is. If you speak to a builder who loves his work, he will tell you that each home feels different and turns out differently even though they may have the same floor plan.

The three people that influenced my life the most were my mother, grandmother and an old Chinese friend Lynette. They all taught me about the three most important things in the home.

1. YOUR BED

Make your bed every morning. Do not leave the house without making your bed. If you make your bed every morning it will help your brain function better and is a form of self-discipline. It's also important to have a beautiful bed, with beautiful covers and accessories. When it's made stand back and look at the finished job. It is a complete task that stays that way until you sleep again. It also sends your brain happy thoughts to start the day if you have colours and a bed you love.

A good quality mattress and pillows is essential. Don't fall into the trap of buying cheap synthetic pillows, the filling is full of chemicals and attracts dust. There are so many natural good quality pillows available that you have no excuse for buying inferior quality. Bed linen is also very important. NEVER EVER buy polyester sheets. They are coated with or have formaldehyde as part of the fibre and give off chemical residue when connected to body heat. Formaldehyde can cause headaches, skin rashes, sinus problems, fatigue, and insomnia. Cotton, polyester mix is just as bad. Keep your phone and other electricals out of the bedroom if you can as the digital, electrical and Wi Fi frequency will affect your sleep.

2. THE DINING ROOM TABLE

It's important to have a happy dining table, a place where everyone can sit, feel comfortable and enjoy the company of friends and family. There is nothing like good food, good company and good conversation. One of my best memories is of my Grandmother's Christmas dinners in her formal dining room with all the family. Everyone was happy, hungry and knew the food would be the best. If we just went to visit we would sit at the kitchen table for lunch or dinner among the fantastic cooking smells, cousins and good food. We would be hungry, noisy and messy and that was ok. I truly believe that if we have a loving feeling for the food we eat and create a happy place to eat it the food is more nutritious and nourishing. My last trip to New York was full of fun and adventure, I ate lots of foods that I normally could not eat, and had no side effects. I truly believe this was because of my mindset of being happy, on holiday, no obligations and stress free.

WHAT YOU EAT TODAY
WALKS AND TALKS TOMORROW.

WHAT YOU THINK TODAY
CREATES YOUR WORLD TOMORROW.

---

3. THE BATH TUB

What is a house without a bath tub and what is life without long luxurious baths, bath salts and bubbles? Children love to have a bath with bubbles and toys. Babies sleep better after a warm bath. There is a certain healing that occurs when you take the time to have a warm bath with healing salts or oils.

Being horizontal in water is relaxing and takes the weight off your limbs.

Baths with organic powdered goats milk and essential oils can help relieve skin conditions.

A hot bath with salts can help with muscle pain.

Warm baths before bed produce better more relaxed sleep.

Relaxing the mind, body, spirit will allow your intuition to flow.

Candles and meditation can help create calmness and inner peace.

A bath before bed is better than television for your head.

Just before you have finished your bath and while you are still laying down, visualise your aches and pains and all the negativity from the day leaving your body and going down the plughole with the water as the bath empties.

For those good at visualisation another great process with your eyes closed is:

Imagine a small cloud above your head. It's held together by lots of threads, they can be plain or coloured. These threads represent all the things you are worried or concerned about. The cloud is full of your concerns and stresses. Imagine the hand of an Angel appearing and removing the threads one at a time. When all the threads are removed, the cloud falls apart and disappears and so do your concerns. Thank your Angel.

This process won't solve your concerns but it may help you have a better night sleep so you can wake up more motivated and clear about how to create change.

RESPECT OTHER PEOPLE

To be able to respect others we must respect ourselves. We lose respect for partners, friends, family and the human race because we do not understand their actions and reactions. If someone doesn't act how we perceive they should then we pass a judgement and lose respect without even knowing the emotion or reason behind the reaction. Most teenagers rebel and do stupid things to punish their parents because the parent says NO. I believe there is a basic universal law that says we must love and respect each other and all things in the universe, but I also believe we have a choice whether we like them or not. I loved and respected my mother but I certainly did not always like how she acted and often did not like her as a person. There are people out there who act and live differently to how you may perceive good people should act. This doesn't mean you should judge them. You have a choice about respecting their life and how they choose to live.

We cannot change anyone; they are who they are meant to be for this life journey. I do believe there is always a possibility we can inspire them to choose an easier path, but the choice must be theirs. The harder you push someone to change the stronger they will be in that negative state of mind because they think you have an opinion of them and its negative. They will not understand that you care more about their future than they do. All they will see is the anger and criticism that is projected from you to them. It is a waste of time to care about someone else's future more than they do. Taking a step back and respecting their space is the best way to save your own sanity and emotional wellbeing. It also gives them back their own personal power that they may have lost because you are trying to control their life. By respecting yourself you make your wellbeing a priority. You no longer go out of your way to do for others while putting your own life on hold.

One of the most powerful secrets I learned from Orlando was that self-respect is a very powerful tool, and that it's ok to step back and let others live their own life. I realised that he respected himself and his life enough to be able to ignore media trivia and not take it personally. Every time I spent time with him he was always happy and excited about the future. He is extremely intuitive and I believe he has a perfect first impression of people when he meets them. He very quickly figures out if they are real or not.

I believe Gratitude and Respect are cousins - they are related. How many of you ever stop and consider the physical, mental, or emotional pain your parents have endured? How many of you have ever sat down and asked your mother about your own birth? I have learned over the years from spiritual healing and kinesiology that the birthing process and how you enter this world makes a big impact on how you feel about yourself. Even thoughts from your mother while you were in the womb will be in your subconscious. Children who are adopted have the biggest burden to carry, after all, if their own parents didn't love them enough to keep them and love them how can they possibly love and accept themselves as being perfect when they entered this world. The feeling of being grateful takes away the need to be judgemental. It also takes away resentment and anger.

If you have a negative relationship with anyone because of how they treat you, then you need to step back and look at how you treat yourself. People will always do to you what you do to yourself; they will treat you how you treat yourself. If you respect yourself physically, spiritually, mentally and financially others will see that energy reflected in your aura and treat you accordingly. Many years ago, I had a friend who was from Holland. She was quite elderly and a little eccentric. She had migrated to Australia after the second world war. Quite often she would tell me stories about how her village had been taken over by the German army and how the survivors had been thrown and locked in the sewerage tunnels under the town. The children would escape and steal food for everyone and that's how they survived. The fear of that trauma never left her and was never far from her memory. That experience changed her life forever but she never let it stop her from living a full and passionate life. Her passion was travel, she would say repeatedly when she was very old "they can take away my home, they can take away everything I own, but they can never take away my memories of the things that have made me happy and of the places I have travelled to and the wondrous things I have experienced. That is the secret of life. When you understand this you can survive anything." She never allowed her past to make her a victim, she loved and respected the world she lived in and was grateful to just be alive, which allowed her to experience freedom to travel the world. She was also one of the first women in Holland to wear a bikini. It was her gratitude for just being alive and surviving that gave her freedom. She never spoke angry words about the experience, she talked about the food she found and was grateful.

One thing I learned from Reiki and Landmark Education is that it took me out of the context that life is all about me and helped me understand that if I look at the effect of life on other people and how they may be feeling then I will have a better understanding of who I am. It's not always about you, and when you have that realisation about life you begin to respect everything you have a little more. Some of the realities I have learnt are: drug addicts don't use drugs to hurt their family or themselves. They use drugs to dull the emotional pain that they can't express and don't know how to heal. As a human it's hard not to take things to heart, you just need to keep saying to yourself "Everything is ok, they are upset with themselves, it's their issue I can't make this about me, I just need to step back and let the dust settle, I need to create boundaries that show I respect myself."

Your respect boundaries need to work for you. It is a good idea to make a list of what you can live with, and a list of what you cannot live with. The list needs to serve you and your best interest.

Chapter 7

PASSION

Luke Gottwald

Chapter 7

PASSION

Luke Gottwald

Never underestimate the power of passion.

LOVE WHAT YOU DO, DO WHAT YOU LOVE

To live without passion is to live without purpose.

Luke, or better known as Dr. Luke, has an amazing gift. He can write music and lyrics. He is loved and respected by everyone who meets him in the music industry and in everyday life. He has a long list of successful hits with Katy Perry, Pitbull, Miley Cyrus, Britney Spears, Jessie J, Nicki Minaj, just to name a few. The list of his successful hit songs is endless.

> “ There is something special and different about famous people. They have a presence, a shiny light that separates them from the mundane. ”

When I first met Luke I didn't realise who he was, but he definitely had a presence about him I had never encountered before and I knew he was destined for amazing things and a much bigger life than he had ever anticipated for himself. He was a friend of one of my clients. My first impression was that he was a gentle soul who loved his work and cared deeply for his friends and family. I felt he was a little unsure about me, maybe because of my straight to the point Australian attitude. We met on my very first trip to Los Angeles, an occasion I will never forget. I felt a strong spiritual connection at that first meeting and still feel it today. He is a very old soul with special spiritual qualities that I believe connect him to his intuitive creative ability and he is naturally gifted.

He is filled with passion for his work, and it is so powerful that it drives him to be the best he can possibly be at his craft. He surrounds himself with a group of talented and passionate people that feel the same as he does about their work. I remember one day he was having human thoughts about his work and I said to him as a motivation, "If you ever doubt your work and what you do, just think of your songs revolving around the world making people happy. Every second of every day someone listens to one of your songs and feels better. You change people's thoughts and energy because they sing, dance, or just listen to your music and feel a whole lot better about everything." How many of you out there sang along with Katy Perry and ROAR? I know I did. Luke taught me about the power of passion. He is passionate about every aspect of his life, his work, employees, home, family and helping others.

> “ To have passion for anything you must be able to dream. ”

There are three kinds of dreamers in the world. There are those who dream of creating an amazing life, they say their affirmations every day and go to bed at night dreaming of their wonderful life. Ten years later they look at their life and realise there is no creation of the dream. They are the night dreamers. The procrastinators, the mundane who have come to earth to have an existence living in a state of survival, always wishing and hoping their life will someday turn a corner and be better.

Then there are the day dreamers, they who turn their dream into reality. They have a passion and a reason for living. They inspire others to believe in their dream and aspire to become masters of their own destiny. They are the powerful energies who live life with passion and purpose. It may be to have the dream home and family, the career, or to save the world in some way. Then there is the third kind of dreamer. They dream 24 hours a day. The day dream is created as a reality, they take action, inspire others to be involved and then they dream at night often astral travelling to have a glimpse of the future, meditating to create a dream state so they can use visualisation, asking their intuition for help and guidance and also putting their brain to work while they sleep to give them the ultimate answers. The results of using every facility available enables them to have a reality they live every day but also to have a passionate dream that is an altered reality which is their future. The dream for the future will manifest itself because it is real in their mind and not just a picture or a thought. A passion begins as a thought that comes from the heart and turns into a dream. The dream then becomes the reason for being passionate.

At some point in your life you need to say there is no way, there is no way, MY DREAM WILL BECOME A REALITY. Friends and family will tell you it's not possible, don't be stupid, stay in the job or relationship you have, at least it's safe and there is a wage coming in each week, better the devil you know than the one you don't.

Every child has a dream of being something, fireman, spaceman, policeman, saving whales, being a famous, actor, singer, dancer. You just need to be in a class room with ten year old children to hear the belief and excitement. They have no doubt that they can be who they dream to be. It's the teachers, parents, older children and society that steal their ability to dream. It takes away their belief in themselves. Maybe they are taught that they are not clever enough, that there is not enough money to pay for lessons, their siblings are more important, who knows the reason. Only you know why you didn't follow your own dream. I was very lucky, as I grew older my mother became more of a friend. We still had our moments, but I could talk to her about what I wanted to do. Her answer was always, "You can't be any worse off than you are now and really, you have nothing to lose, so you should go ahead and give it a try. I don't see why you can't do what you want." This gave me something to hold on to. I have always followed my dreams.

I have been in Luke's presence when he has asked how a project is going. The answer was it isn't finished and this was after he had worked until 2 or 3 in the morning on it. I saw the look on his face as he digested the answer and instead of reacting which is what most bosses would do, he calmly called everyone together and discussed how they should finish off the project. He knew there was a way, I could see it on his face, it was like he turned on a little computer that has solutions not reactions. I have also been in the presence of other powerful people who think the same; they have a passion and they never give up. Sometimes the business or career may not always be the passion, but it will provide them with the stable funds to follow their passion as a hobby or to start their passion as a business. Miranda Kerr did this with her skin care range KORA. She worked with her modelling while following her passion to have a skin care range that is unique, organic and makes a difference.

Imagine the world if Sir Richard Branson had not followed his passion, how empty would he feel today if he had given up, if he had listened to the people who said it's not possible. Jennifer Lopez is another classic example of, you can't do that you will fail. I'm sure the world is a better place because she never listened to the negative words spoken to her.

One reason your friends, family, partners will talk you out of following your passion is because they are afraid you will become different. They are used to you how you are and are afraid that if you are powerful, successful, and free from the restrictions of society you may not need them anymore, that you will outgrow them. They may not realise they are thinking this but I assure you it is true and on a deep subconscious level. Fear of losing you and of you failing will be their motive to talk you out of it. Most parents are experts at doing this. It's not because they don't love you, it's because they are afraid you will fail and if you do then that means that they as parents are a failure, because there is something that they should have taught you and they didn't. The only pattern they have to draft your life by is their own. Their successes and failures are the foundation for your success. And you saw this growing up so it will all be registered in your brain as a way of survival. You will take on your father or mother's disappointment, responsibility or whatever they expressed when they were in survival. How many of you do whatever to please your parents to gain their approval? If you don't conform you are the outcast, the one who bends the rules, even your siblings give up on you and judge you by their own standards of what they think you should be doing to conform to society. When you have found your passion which you believe to be your destiny, stay focused on that path. Sometimes when we are multitalented we become side tracked by other opportunities.

THE BIG PICTURE

The truth about passion is that it may not be what you are good at; it's about creating your dream; what you know in your heart to be your destiny.

I recently met a young man who came to me to sort out his career. He had a job in retail which paid good wages and the staff were friendly. He had no reason to leave, he could stay there for 10 years if he wanted to. He was passionate about reiki and helping people in some way so I told him I would share as much of my knowledge as I could about whatever he wanted to know. I also introduced him to other healing modalities so he could experience how other practitioners work. For almost 12 months he experienced different growth transformations. He had started working out at the gym a few years previously to be fit and healthy and lose weight. He stayed committed to working out and never doubted himself in that area. He came to me with a dream of opening a centre for people to heal and learn; I could tell by the look in his eyes that he had no idea how it would happen. By believing in and following his dream and intuition he has found his true passion with the possible outcome of completing his goal at some stage in the future. He studied healing modalities which he felt were right for him and gradually started his life transformation. He is still working in the same retail position. I hadn't heard from him for a while and wondered what he was up to so I sent him a text message. He immediately called me and told me about his realisation that he wanted to become a holistic health coach and that he had started a personal trainer course on his days off. He discussed the possibility of combining the spiritual health techniques he would learn with personal fitness. He had also discovered the importance of breath and breathing techniques, so I shared my connections with him in that area. I know he will fulfil his dream, while embracing his passion. He is creating one goal at a time, one step at a time, always with his eye on the big picture.

> "I alone cannot change the world,
> but I can cast a stone across the waters to
> create many ripples."
>
> MOTHER TERESA

My gift is clairvoyance, reading people and helping people so the world is a better place. I believe in the ripple effect. If you help one person, maybe a father and his life is improved and he is less stressed and happier, his work colleagues, family, neighbours, other drivers on the road, even the girl he buys his coffee or lunch from have a better day because he is polite, humorous and shares his happiness with everyone he meets. Getting back to PASSION, I believe one of the clever things to do is find what you are very good at and make that your career (and it's something you will usually like because it's easy), make your money at that career to pay the bills, study your passion, enjoy life and when you have set yourself up start working with your passion part time. That way your brain doesn't try to talk you out of creating a passionate life because there is no money coming in and you are stressed to the max and setting yourself up to fail just so your intelligent brain can be smarter than your intuition. The secret to working with your intuition is to let your intelligence think it is in control.

When you have a dream or a passion and you want to turn it into a reality, it's easy to think in your mind what you want to create, but sometimes your brain will not let you see how to create a plan that will work.

The steps to creating…tell as few people as possible about your plan for your passion until you are ready to go ahead with firm commitment and a plan of action. This will save you a lot of upset because someone else has an opinion of you or your idea. It can also dissipate your energy if you spread it around too much and let's face it, sometimes other people like your idea and run with it for themselves and act like it was their genius that created the possibility in the first place. You can also use this technique for small goals as well as for the big one. You can make this simple with a few steps or you can have a hundred steps if you like. Add pictures but not too many. Read the goals aloud to yourself every day and cross off the completed goal or replace it with something else you have discovered you need to do to create the desired result.

You can use these steps for anything, from how to cook to opening your own restaurant:

1. Sit quietly and visualise what you would like to create, then ask yourself if there is any reason why you cannot have this outcome.

2. Then in your mind see yourself being that person, living that life. Being with like-minded people, driving that car, having your own business, saving dolphins, creating your own product. Whatever the passion.

3. Then ask yourself who would not want you to be that person, just be aware of who comes into your mind and write their name down. There may be more than one person. Ask yourself why they may not want you to change your life and what it will mean to them. This will help you deal with any negative comments made by anyone. Try not to discuss your plans when you are with these people. Remember they may love you and not want to see you hurt or disappointed or they may be jealous because they never had the courage to follow their heart.

4. Find a mentor, they may be someone you know or can be someone you admire. Study them and follow their plan of action; if they are successful you have a proven path to follow. You will find it gives you inspiration to know someone else has been where you are and come out the other side. Research their life, learn how they act, live, treat people and even speak.

5. Look at other people who are doing what you want to do and decide what you like or dislike about how they operate. List the things you

don't like and make sure you don't do them. List the things you love and add them to your plan.

6. Make a vision board of your plan of action. Have lots of small circles on the board with one large circle in the middle. Number the small circles one to ten or twenty depending on the steps you need to take to create the goal. Each small circle represents the actions you need to take to create the big goal which is the big circle. This process works for everything. The trick is to make your brain think the big goal is easy.

7. Buy a look good, feel good exercise book and use it as your vision book. Take this book with you for notes and new ideas as well as keeping you motivated. You can use a twelve month plan, creating a chapter for each month. Stick lots of pictures in for each month as well as the small daily, weekly or monthly goals.

Don't worry about what other people think, and don't worry about what YOU think other people think. Follow your passion and create your dream. This goes both ways, most of the time, other people are not living the life you think they are, they may act happy and successful, but underneath may be sad and feel a failure. The choice is yours. You may embrace your own empowerment by drawing a line in the sand and say no more of this old outdated way of existing. You have a dream for yourself, as you fulfil that dream you will lift others from survival to a place of motivation and dreaming. Know who you are and who you can aspire to be with all the commitment and diligence you can pull from your soul to build yourself a new life, a new way of living from the heart and not from your environment and those who coexist in that environment with you. Those who coexist with you control and manipulate you to their way of assuming that's what is best for you, sometimes with love and sometimes from their fear for themselves and their own failures. You are not your environment because that is where you live or because others say so. You are no longer the child who grew up in a particular circumstance. Make time for quiet contemplation and planning, being aware of your surroundings and the people in your life. Always ask yourself does this job, person, action or decision contribute in a positive way to my future or will it play a part in sabotaging my dream in some way? If the answer is positive remember, you will also impact the lives of others in a positive way.

Your destiny may be written but you are the owner of the story that travels beside your destiny. Commit to writing your own new story. Let go of the past chapters and anyone else's script. They no longer serve your purpose and are not truthful about who you truly are. It's important to be free of WANT. It is the desire of self-destruction. If you want wealth, marriage, success it will consume your spirit and you will transcend from someone who has a dream to someone driven to succeed and cannot bear the thought of failure and losing your material and worldly possessions. This fear and need will make you cross the line of truth and integrity, creating the false world that you will exist in. If you replace the want and only create what you need, you will have the same result minus the stress and anger. Men usually seek power and relate it to wealth. Women sometimes seek power to be free of everyone.

Chapter 8

I WISH I HAD

Bringing it all together

Chapter 8

I WISH I HAD

Bringing it all together

We are all different, yet the same. An office worker in New York may live their life parallel to an office worker in London who lives their life parallel to someone in Sydney. They are born, grow up, work in an office, get married, have a family, grow old and just live life. The same could be said for a fisherman in the Gulf of Mexico, compared to a fisherman in Perth, Australia. They are fisherman, have families, know the ocean and its secrets, understand their journey and that's the life they live. Airline pilots around the world live parallel to each other; they have the same passion, probably pass each other in the sky and never even think about who the other person truly is. They are pilots running parallel along the same path. They get married, have families, live their life as pilots and retire. Just like the office worker and the fisherman, they exist in their own world creating their own life to live as a human with the purpose of living, experiencing and enjoying life. There are billions of people who just live parallel lives; they don't question their spiritual existence or search endlessly to find answers. They are not looking for the missing link.

I have questioned why I have worked with certain famous people around the world and realise the celebrities who have found me are different. They search for self-realisation. Not all famous people have this desire. Many of them live parallel or mundane lives. They are still shiny and special but they live in existence not awareness. The same as the office worker and the pilot. I have met many of you over the years who are special. You come to me not understanding your journey because you have always felt different and special in some way but have not had the tools or understanding to embrace who you are. This need evokes the journey of the spirit to search until you find like-minded people and self-realisation. In times past you have experienced a connection to spirit through religion of some sort, but since the decline of belief in the people who run religion, there has been a decline in the ability to trust churches and those who run them. This creates the desire to find the connection in a different way. This has brought about the need for spiritual growth and self-help gurus and empires allowing you the connection to continue your search knowing you are not alone.

Self-awareness and spiritual growth that comes with truth of self, creates the possibility of living a happy and fulfilled life without the 'I wish I had.' I always say it is too late when you are dead to say I wish I had allowed myself to truly love or to let go of the fear and embrace my own success. I wish I had cared about my friends, expressed love for my family and shared my life with them instead of hiding behind my fear of allowing myself to be who I truly am because I am afraid they will laugh at me or not love me. I wish I had followed my dream and become a teacher, pilot, nurse, actress or whatever. To remember that you are only here for such a short time and that you are special and choose or choose not to have awareness. Whatever your choice, you will live your life and then you will leave the planet and become a memory. The memory people have of you is your choice as well. So why not create the best and most powerful memory you possibly can.

My next book THE HIDDEN TRUTH will give you an even deeper perspective into who you are as a spiritual human. It will be a total healing and transformational workbook. If you would like to be advised about the release date check in on my website www.jeanclare.com.au.

7 REASONS WHY I AM SPECIAL

Make lists of the following and add pictures

7 GOALS I HAVE COMPLETED

MY 7 FAVOURITE CELEBRITIES

7 METHODS I USE TO STAY MOTIVATED

THE 7 THINGS I LOVE ABOUT MYSELF

THE 7 SPECIAL THINGS I NEED TO DO WEEKLY JUST FOR ME

7 FRIENDS/ ASSOCIATES WHO LEAVE ME FEELING MOTIVATED AND INSPIRED

MY 7 FAVOURITE FOODS

7 ANCESTORS/ FAMILY WHO ARE SUCCESSFUL

7 WAYS I AM UNIQUE AND SPECIAL

7 THINGS I WOULD DO TO IMPROVE THE WORLD

7 THINGS I LOVE ABOUT MY HOME

7 PEOPLE WHO LOVE ME UNCONDITIONALLY

7 REASONS I LOVE MY WORK

7 WONDERFUL THINGS I HAVE DONE FOR OTHER PEOPLE

7 THINGS I LOVE ABOUT MY FAMILY

7 CITIES I WOULD LOVE TO VISIT

MY 7 FAVOURITE SONGS

MY WISHES AND DREAMS FOR THE NEXT 7 YEARS

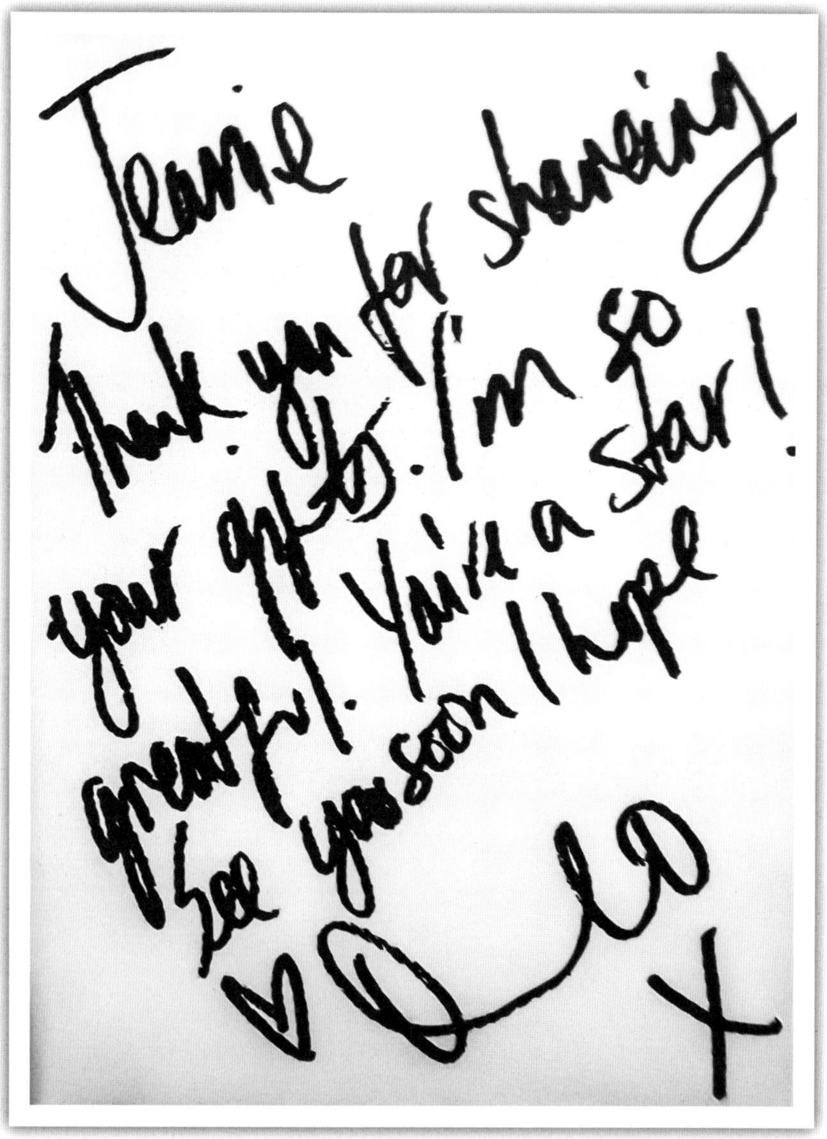
Jeanie
Thank you for sharing your gifts. I'm so greatful. You're a star! See you soon I hope
♥
x

A thank you to JeanClare from Orlando Bloom

Denise Vassi and Jeannine Kasper during a trip to LosAngeles

Jeannine

Yael

Miranda and JeanClare at David Jones Fashion Parade Sydney

Miranda Kerr and JeanClare in Sydney Australia

Orlando and JeanClare at Sawtell Beach Australia

About the Author

JEANCLARE

JeanClare was born in the small town of Coffs Harbour, New South Wales, Australia.

Thanks to her mother and Enid Blyton, she grew up believing enchanted magic was real and to this day still believes that it is possible to pass from one realm of existence to another. This reality allowed the amazing possibility that she could create anything and that all things were possible. By the time she was thirty, with the inherited gifts of clairvoyance, clairsentience and clairaudience, she began the journey into the world of Spiritual Growth and Self-awareness.

JeanClare is an author, entrepreneur, clairvoyant, Reiki Master, teacher, public speaker.

JeanClare has a large client base of actors, models, television personalities, writers, designers, and other professionals in Australia, New Zealand, Tasmania, and the United States of America. They include Miranda Kerr, Orlando Bloom, Yfke Sturm, Jeannine Kaspar, Shelby Stone, Alina Puscau, Jessica Hernandez, Elyse Taylor, Chris

Rios, Jessica James, Luke Gottwald, Pete Everett, Scarlet Vespa, Wendy Matthews, Yael Lilienfeld, Zoe Saldana and many more.

She has travelled and worked throughout Australia, England, Scotland, Ireland, Wales, Holland, Italy, Canada, and the United States of America.

JeanClare is the author of 'Never Give Up' and lives in Tweed Heads, Australia.